2021

Incredible Imaginations

Edited By Sarah Waterhouse

First published in Great Britain in 2021 by:

Young Writers
Remus House
Coltsfoot Drive
Peterborough
PE2 9BF
Telephone: 01733 890066
Website: www.youngwriters.co.uk

All Rights Reserved
Book Design by Ashley Janson
© Copyright Contributors 2021
Softback ISBN 978-1-80015-468-1

Printed and bound in the UK by BookPrintingUK
Website: www.bookprintinguk.com
YB0474E

★ FOREWORD ★

Welcome Reader!

Are you ready to discover weird and wonderful creatures that you'd never even dreamed of?

For Young Writers' latest competition we asked primary school pupils to create a Peculiar Pet of their own invention, and then write a poem about it! They rose to the challenge magnificently and the result is this fantastic collection full of creepy critters and amazing animals!

Here at Young Writers our aim is to encourage creativity in children and to inspire a love of the written word, so it's great to get such an amazing response, with some absolutely fantastic poems. Not only have these young authors created imaginative and inventive animals, they've also crafted wonderful poems to showcase their creations and their writing ability. These poems are brimming with inspiration. The slimiest slitherers, the creepiest crawlers and furriest friends are all brought to life in these pages – you can decide for yourself which ones you'd like as a pet!

I'd like to congratulate all the young authors in this anthology, I hope this inspires them to continue with their creative writing.

★

★

★ CONTENTS ★

Allithwaite CE Primary School, Allithwaite

Abigail Thexton (9)	1
Rosalie Johnson (10)	2
Robert Brown (10)	3
Bo Frankie Myatt (10)	4
Oliver Gonzalez (10)	5
James Hall (10)	6
Alfie Connor (10)	7
Rosie Randall (9)	8
Joe Elson (10)	9
Lacey Turner (11)	10

Chatsworth Primary School, Hounslow

Molly Cross	11
Mohammed Faiz Basha (9)	12
Julia Sierakowska (10)	14
Aarav Praveen (9)	16

Gardners Lane Primary School, Cheltenham

Paige Jackson (10)	17
Lilah Peach (10)	18
Carson Cleal (10)	20
Gracie Gill (10)	21
Daizzy Njoku (10)	22
Lacey Mae (10)	24
Ifra Rahman (10)	25
Jonathan Tarling (10)	26
Melany Del Cid Aguirre (10)	27
Josie Baron (9)	28
Skye Clarke (10)	29

Imogen Granville (9)	30
Katherine Bradley (9)	31
Ruby Harper (9)	32
Gracie Slee (10)	33
Hannah Clarke (10)	34
Sam Montague (9)	35
Harry Dawson (10)	36
Evie Davis (10)	37
Jasmine Loveridge (10)	38
Nacho Comeche Tallester (10)	39
Ayo Gabriel (10)	40
Bobby Locke (10)	41
Mason Mchugh (10)	42
James Holloway (9)	43
Diego Milena (9)	44
Ruby Didcote (10)	45
Tyler-James Finn (10)	46
Shelby Collins Chambers (9)	47
Archie Orpin (9)	48
Layla-Rose Dorling (9)	49
Maisie Hester (10)	50
Oscar Lightstone (9)	51
Jack Aguirre (10)	52

Gillygooley Primary School, Omagh

Emily Hemphill (11)	53
Jack Walker (10)	54
Natasha Elliott (10)	55
Zoey Crankshaw (11)	56
Rachel Nelson (11)	57
Harry McCormack (11)	58
Mark Cousins (11)	59
Emily Mackey (10)	60

Guilden Morden CE Primary Academy, Guilden Morden

Amelie Seymour (10)	61
Freddie Barnes (8)	62
Harrison Catheart (8)	63
Esther Cutler (8)	64
Ophelia Hall (8)	65
Daniel Taran (9)	66
Bethany Maley (11)	67
Ella-Louise Groom (9)	68
Andrew Speed (11)	69
Devon Julyan1 (11)	70

Halewood CE Primary School, Halewood

Fernando Alondia Almeida-Amos (9)	71
Sienna Mutch (9)	72
Lucie Moss (9)	74
Ella-Sofia Hennity (9)	76
Kaitlin Potts (9)	78
Sophie Lloyd (9)	79
Samuel Rooney (9)	80
Ava Stephens (8)	81
Annie Williams (9)	82
Elise McGregor (9)	83
Sophie Dean (8)	84
Joshua Healey (9)	85
Daniel Fitzsimmons (8)	86
Ellie McGregor (9)	87
Daniel Glover (8)	88
Ethan Wells (9)	89
Mae Anders (9)	90
Isla Fearns (9)	91
Oliver Banlin (9)	92
Jake Cardwell (9)	93
Herbie T Webb (8)	94
Charlie Walker (9)	95

Larchfield Primary & Nursery School, Maidenhead

Kalina Walczak (9)	96
Polina Nahimovics (8)	97
Emma Pennington (8)	98
Imaad Rahman (9)	99
Sabeeha Shahzad (9)	100
Sophie Horwood (9)	101
Alexia Pascu (9)	102
Diya Thumsi (8)	103
Julia Miklas (9)	104
Rakshitha Ramesh-Babu (8)	105
Starla Saw (8)	106
Breah Rance (9)	107
Tyler Brench (9)	108
Nithila Suganthan (9)	109
Falisha Khan (8)	110
Jayme Figueira (9)	111
Freddie Branch (9)	112
Anaiza Fernandez (9)	113
Jessie Savage (9)	114
Marina Kemp-Brown (9)	115
Anthony Duffy (9)	116
Layla Clarke (8)	117
Holly Jones (9)	118
Andrew Gillespie (9)	119

Lochnell Primary School, Benderloch

Cameron Clifford (8)	120
Calum Kill (9)	121
Eachan MacDonald (8)	122
Lewis Hart (10)	123
Mirren MacDonald (10)	124
Sam Wilson (9)	125
Grace Stewart (10)	126
Angus Carswell (10)	127
Skyela Stuart (9)	128
Joshua MacNiven (9)	129
Roan Waslidge (10)	130
Dean Cotton (10)	131
Rosie Campbell (10)	132

James Blomfield (11)	133
Christopher MacLaurin (8)	134
Mac Rodwell (11)	135
Lucas Bonniwell (9)	136
Caitlin MacColl (11)	137
Thomas Davies	138
Alice Macdonald (10)	139
James Steward (11)	140
Alasdair Bruce (10)	141
Lewis Shaw (11)	142
Alasdair Bullock (9)	143
Mia Travers (9)	144
Phoebe Lavis-Jones (9)	145
Jackie Stewart (10)	146
Charlie Randle (8)	147
Mia Taylor (10)	148
Lucy Macgregor (9)	149
Ashley Wood (11)	150
Rory Struthers (9)	151
Finlay MacCallum (11)	152
Fraser MacGregor (10)	153

Melvich Primary School, Melvich

Eevie Mackay (11)	154
Callan Mackay (10)	155

Portlethen Primary School, Portlethen

Leah MacPherson (9)	156
Caleb Bremner (10)	157
Mia Vaughan (9)	158
Paulina Kekenmejster (10)	159
Jessica Hope Murray (8)	160
Logan Bonner (9)	161
Hannah Cowie (8)	162
Lotti Szigeti (9)	163
Zuzanna Kalczynska (9)	164
Ryan Stuart Lawie (8)	165
Eva Duminicel (9)	166
Liam Law (10)	167
Freddi Ferguson (9)	168
Rockland Brooks (9)	169

Adi Pazio (9)	170
Baxter Smith (9)	171

Ridgeway Farm CE Academy, Purton

Haadiya Omar (9)	172
Yvette Ncube (9)	173
Jaiyana Gurung (10)	174
Max Bennett (10)	175
Zubin Beach (9)	176
Erin Blackmore (9)	177
Kyra Morgan (10)	178
Leo Clarke (10)	179
Freya Blackmore (9)	180
Vittoria Dos Santos (10)	181
Terrence French (9)	182
Freya Popovic (9)	183
Tinotenda Mundembe (10)	184
Max Keating Ladd (10)	185
Freddie Hall (10)	186
Maisie Debs New (10)	187
Harry Stoddart (10)	188

Rutherglen High School, Campus Lane

Daniel Legan (13)	189
Euan Shevlin (13)	190

St Joseph's Primary School, Antrim

Conor McGarry (10)	191
Lucius McCollum (11)	192

Westray Junior High School, Westray

Melissa Nicolson (9)	193
Mia Pottinger (9)	194
Eiza Dickinson (8)	195
Arun Summers (7)	196
Tanna Groat (9)	197
Millie-Megan Bliss (7)	198

Stewart Rendall (8)	199
Robert Sam Rendall (9)	200
Mason Bain (8)	201
James Groat (7)	202

Wetherby School, London

Shiv Vohra (7)	203
Pedro Aboim (7)	204
Dhilan Besser (7)	205
Raphael Zechner (7)	206
Sebastian Zacharioudakis (7)	207
Jack-Li Woon (7)	208
Lucas Marks (7)	209
Izaia Porseous (7)	210
Sebastian Lavers (7)	211
Alexander Grimm (7)	212
Federico Assetto (7)	213
Sam Chebaklo (6)	214
Henry Abraham (7)	215
Leo Head (7)	216
Wenty Beaumont (7)	217
Epaminondas George Embiricos (7)	218
Tristan Ysenburg (7)	219
Leo Larsson (7)	220
Teddy Lazari (7)	221
Freddie Jilla (7)	222
Alexander Michael Haddad (7)	223
Farrukh Sheikh (7)	224
Bartle Frankopan	225
Lucas Zammitt (7)	226
Rupert Nicholls (7)	227
Billy Marsh (7)	228
Hamzah Sharaf (6)	229
Conrad Parkin (6)	230
Edward Abboud (7)	231
Xander Petersen (7)	232
Yuveer Goenka (7)	233
Alex Taylor (7)	234
Philip Teboul (7)	235
Maxi Fatemi (7)	236
Alexander Whyatt (7)	237
Rex Richardson (7)	238
Arthur Lindback (7)	239
Theo Gladkov (6)	240
Eduardo Rio (7)	241
Hugh Crossley Wright (7)	242
Freddy Bakewell (6)	243

THE POEMS

The Unfermershark

It lives in the sea
If you are wise
You will know it's not a disguise.
Its scales are diamonds at night.
It warms the sea day and night.
It hunts at the start of the night.

It eats humans, they taste like a delight
It cuts the middle and eats the insides, then out
But if you light a torch, then it shows
You won't hear it
It will let you on its back.
Do not fear if it rears
It will love you and protect you forever.

Abigail Thexton (9)
Allithwaite CE Primary School, Allithwaite

Fanglse

F anglse, threatening beast, eating mice.
A nimal with a vicious bite.
N ever get lost or you would have a fright.
"G oing somewhere?" she would say before a killing fight.
L etting a cat in at night, claws and scares are a fright.
S eeing mice flying through the sky, knowing they're about to die.
E ven if you see this cat, remember that she's not a cat!

Rosalie Johnson (10)
Allithwaite CE Primary School, Allithwaite

My Incredible Rhino-Budgie

No pet is better than Rhino-Budgie,
He's so sweet and squidgy.
He's cute in the light,
But a rockstar at night.

He gets his guitar
And plays with Shalamar,
He goes to Glastonbury
And normally eats a strawberry.

And after night, he goes in his cage,
Not really in a rage.
He's fast asleep,
Not making a peep,
Waiting for his next gig,
Wearing a wig...

Robert Brown (10)
Allithwaite CE Primary School, Allithwaite

My Hedgbunny

No such thing like a Hedgbunny,
Always out when it's sunny,
Hidden away when dark at night,
Don't stroke it otherwise your hand will be a sight!

This Hedgbunny is quite fierce,
Don't anger it or it can give you a pierce,
But let me make sure you're aware
This is *my* Hedgbunny *everywhere.*

Bo Frankie Myatt (10)
Allithwaite CE Primary School, Allithwaite

T-Eleosalapard

The T-Eleosalapard
It eats telephones
And it is coming for your bones
And next are your phones
He likes parties
And he is addicted to palm trees.

How are you going to tame this monster?
It's got elephant ears and leopard whiskers, T-rex claws
And it destroys boars
And he also has really loud roars!

Oliver Gonzalez (10)
Allithwaite CE Primary School, Allithwaite

My Sharkatan: The Zookeeper For Humans

My amazing Sharkatan,
No one knows why but he really hates man,
He locks them in a zoo
And makes them wear tutus.

He's as large as the Empire State,
As tall as they can make,
His rainbow scales glimmer in the light
And everyone bows before his unholy might.

James Hall (10)
Allithwaite CE Primary School, Allithwaite

Budgsurbephoenix

This is my pet
By day, he is a normal budgie
But at night, you would not want to pat
Since at night, it's a fright
He turns into...
Budgsurbephoenix.
It barks like a dog
And tweets like a budgie also
We go on a ride to the moon
Every single night.

Alfie Connor (10)
Allithwaite CE Primary School, Allithwaite

Happy Life

Nobody loves me!
But one day
My wish actually came true
I got an owner so now I'm not ashamed

We go out, she hops on my back
We fly away, soon we land
In the sand.
So now we live a happy life.

Rosie Randall (9)
Allithwaite CE Primary School, Allithwaite

My Mamoraptor

My pet is wonderful,
The Mamoraptor is great,
He may be dangerous
But he can be a mate.

He looks frightening
Because he is furry,
But he is not unfriendly
For he can be merry.

Joe Elson (10)
Allithwaite CE Primary School, Allithwaite

HorBudgie Duckerdog

If I had HorBudgie Duckerdog
I would jump on his back
Then go to the beach
I would run around with him
I would go swimming with him
I would go in a field with him.

Lacey Turner (11)
Allithwaite CE Primary School, Allithwaite

My Peculiar Pet

Be scared, be aware, be cautious of his lair
Colin the cobra, my peculiar pet
He slithers up the house to let
His unusual friends in who are wet
Be scared, be aware, be cautious of his lair
He roams the land when you're asleep
And lies in the cupboard, deciding to weep
Be scared, be aware, be cautious of his lair
You can see the glint in his eye when he's ready to scare
You can taste the fear when you see his fangs
Look up to the light fitting where he hangs
Be scared, be aware, be cautious of his lair
When he sleeps, shut the door
Because he will be wanting more
Put his food down and don't let mice scamper on the floor...

Molly Cross
Chatsworth Primary School, Hounslow

Super Sans The Skeleton Snake

Super Sans the skeleton snake
Peers upon its prey
It will rip and tear
It has poisonous fangs to catch its prey
It is not good at dodging and is very strong
It has lightning on its eye.

It will spend its days climbing up trees and scaring monkeys.
Hiss, hiss it goes and slithers to its prey
With poisonous fangs, he poisons his food
And with a poisonous long tongue living in its mouth that is as long as a jet,
Ouch, ouch, it captures its prey.
Slam, slam, it throws its enemies onto the floor with its tongue
Super Sans the skeleton snake is the new mischievous snake.

Be scared, very scared of the stealthy snake
For its tongue is as sharp as a knife with a jagged point
Its eyes are full of death.
So be scared, be very scared,

Be scared, very scared of the stealthy snake
For its hisses and snarls are terribly loud
Petrified people flee from it.
So be scared, very scared,

Be scared, very scared of the stealthy snake
For he flits between the dark and slithers slyly
His tail scrapes the ground.
So be scared, be very scared

Be scared, be scared of the stealthy snake
For it is very cheeky,
And steals from everyone.
So be scared, be very scared...

Mohammed Faiz Basha (9)
Chatsworth Primary School, Hounslow

The Adventures Of Zephna The Sausage Cat

Zephna, Zephna, the sausage cat
She's unusual, I'll tell you that!
I'm her owner, she's my best friend
But I bet you the fun will never end!

I love her so much even if she's long
From the day I saw her, she was cute all along
We've had adventures better than the rest
And our journeys were better than the best

Journeys better than Dashing Dog's
And even better than Hamster McHog's
One day, we travelled to the beach
There was a nice shell too high to reach

Then Zephna grabbed the shell for me
That made me awfully happy
How did she get it from way up there?
We make such a fantastic pair

Once, I even skydived with her
On the way down, it messed up her fur
We went to the forest to climb trees
When we got to the top, we enjoyed the breeze

I'd like to go on like our tea with a Lord
But the list goes on, so you'd get bored!
Goodbye, we're off to make a den
When we have time, we will see you again.

Julia Sierakowska (10)
Chatsworth Primary School, Hounslow

Is There A Dogosaur At Your Door?

The dogosaur stamping at your door
Stomps so boisterous you'd fall to the floor

Eats all day
This guy won't have to pay

This deadly dogosaur goes to sleep
You don't want to take a peep

Wakes up, stomps some more
It's like an elephant is shaking a door

Swings its mighty tail, make sure to duck
Out of any pets, this one will have good luck...

Aarav Praveen (9)
Chatsworth Primary School, Hounslow

Tiger Poem

This tiger is black and white
With a very dangerous bite,
This tiger has a peculiar personality
And what he does in the day you will never believe,
He cleans my house for when I come home
And he does my washing too,
In his free time, he likes to go skydiving,
Every night he reads us books, but he forgets he can't talk,
So he just says, "Bark, bark... b... bark!"
After an hour of reading,
He falls into a deep, deep sleep,
But thirty minutes later,
He wakes up and starts to sweep the house while the family are asleep.
Breakfast is made by the time we are awake,
And the house is tidy too.
He becomes a tiger once again,
For a while until two.

Paige Jackson (10)
Gardners Lane Primary School, Cheltenham

Daniel The Donkey Musician

D ancing all night long
A pples are his favourite food
N obody plays the piano better than him
I t is fun being a musician
E verybody loves it when Daniel breakdancing
L eaving the piano was not easy

T he crowd goes wild when Daniel plays jazz
H e loves his job
E very night he writes a new song

D oesn't everybody want a dancing donkey?
O ne of Daniel's favourite movies is Shrek
N ot everybody has a talking, dancing donkey
K ing Dennis of Donkey Town loves Daniel's music
E dward the elephant is Daniel's best friend
Y esterday we went to the show.

M any people enjoy Daniel's music
U mbrellas scare Daniel, no one knows why
S unday is Daniel's favourite day
I t is Daniel's dream to live in Paris
C harlie the cat has been mean to Daniel since 2006
I t is fun being Daniel's owner
A nybody is lucky to be Daniel's friend
N ever tell Daniel no (he will do it anyway!)

Lilah Peach (10)
Gardners Lane Primary School, Cheltenham

My Crazy Bulldog

My black bulldog does particular things,
Like skydiving on Monday,
He falls from a great height up in the air,
What a great dare!
Tuesday is the day that he goes to read
To all the children at school,
They do comprehensions all day
And he arrives home at four.
Wednesday is his first day off,
He's off for the rest of the week,
Playing video games in his dorm
One round he finally won,
Mashing the controller buttons like a raging bull
He only completed level one,
All the other days he dances and plays
With his owner at home,
They play basketball and
Football, they also play catch with his
Little dog friends at the park.

Carson Cleal (10)
Gardners Lane Primary School, Cheltenham

Coco The Bossy Dog

Coco is my dog, a little weird dog
She does the cooking and
One-hour long reading
She talks in woofs
That we don't know

Storing things upon her throne
We wish we knew what to do
But Coco is the boss of you
For dinner frozen meals

You don't know what is for breakfast
Coco jumps
When it's reading time at night
We have our frozen meals

She slips her glasses onto her head
After an hour, we are asleep
She is the boss when Mom and Dad are out
For a week

So, that's my dog, Coco Miss Bossy
My boss dog that I treasure.

Gracie Gill (10)
Gardners Lane Primary School, Cheltenham

The Brave Gardener

This gardener is a furry dog.
He strokes his plants
And eats his log.

Nobody knows his identity
And nobody knows he speaks

His demeanour changes
With human beings
(And he seems to stop speaking English).

A cat comes chasing him left to right
Trying to distract him
From his plants.

At night-time, he ends up
Protecting his plants
From his prey
That like to feast

When it is night-time
His owners look for him
He has a secret way
Where he sleeps.

Inside the passageway
Sometimes he has a party
When he protects his plants
From different prey.

Daizzy Njoku (10)
Gardners Lane Primary School, Cheltenham

Tilly Dog

In our house, it is not normal
In the morning when I woke up

I saw my dog putting on my make-up
She also wears my clothes and shoes
When no one knows, she goes on her phone

And calls her friends
She also has a dog party

But when you turn back around
She turns back into being a lazy dog

But she is not so lazy when food is around.

When Tilly gets excited
She starts climbing the walls and even flying!
Around, smashing glass.

One time, I caught her paw-handed
Going into the fridge and eating all of my doughnuts.

Lacey Mae (10)
Gardners Lane Primary School, Cheltenham

A Peculiar Tiger

T iger the tiger can drive, but people don't trust him. To talk to, he squeaks which is quite odd
I ntelligent, the tiger is pretty smart when he arrives at school to learn science and English.
G orgeous, the tiger takes off his orange and black stripes, his body is all black like a panther.
E xcitable, the tiger can get overexcited sometimes, like when he discovered a recipe, he screamed!
R easonable, the tiger can get anything he wants as he has his reasons. One time he had been given a scooter, instead of using it normally, he used it upside down!

Ifra Rahman (10)
Gardners Lane Primary School, Cheltenham

The Skipping Dog

This is my house with a little dog,
He washes up after dinner.

He drives like a maniac to work,
Then he drops into the library
And reads books about tigers.

On a Monday, he goes to school
Where he learns maths and skipping.

On a Tuesday, he returns to study his
Favourite subject - English.

On a Wednesday, he works at a
Garden centre.

On a Thursday and Friday, he has a day off
And he flies around the house.

The weekend is just for his painting.

Jonathan Tarling (10)
Gardners Lane Primary School, Cheltenham

The Cat Keera

He goes to the park,
Driving in his car like he always does.

He likes to run all the time,
But he prefers to drive his monster truck.

When he arrives at home, he eats his favourite pizza
And puts his favourite clothes on.

When I go to my room,
He goes with his friends to a party with Selena Gomez

And when I come back,
He is still at a party with his friends.

He takes me to the beach in his monster truck
And he makes a party like he always does.

Melany Del Cid Aguirre (10)
Gardners Lane Primary School, Cheltenham

Scaly The Camouflage Snake

This is my camouflage snake,
She has always seemed to like the bright blue lake.

So when you take her out,
She will camouflage and make you shout!

Sometimes she will make
Herself look like a big fat juicy steak.

This pet has extremely cool skin,
It hides her so well, you need to shout, "Okay, you win!"
My stupid brother Jake
Is scared of my amazing snake
Scaly the snake is the best pet ever,
As long as you don't put her in leather.

Josie Baron (9)
Gardners Lane Primary School, Cheltenham

Budgies

Once, they escaped from their cage
They flew all over the room

Bumping into windows
As if they couldn't see.

Constant tweeting
All day - silence at night.

Feathers of blue, grey,
White, black and yellow.

They swoop down
And steal food from us.

They are active like a fitness group
Flapping wings like arms.

They dance
As they twist and turn

They rest back on their perch.

Skye Clarke (10)
Gardners Lane Primary School, Cheltenham

A Musical Guinea Pig

My guinea pig is so cute,
She thinks that she can play the small red flute.

My guinea pig buys a mini orange wig
Before she books a load of gigs.

She squeaks a lot to let you know
The gig is starting, get up, don't moan.

Cherry likes to play her bright red flute
While eating lots of juicy green mango fruit.

A cuddly guinea pig is an amazing pet
Just don't let them do your hair, please don't forget!

Imogen Granville (9)
Gardners Lane Primary School, Cheltenham

Story Of The Froglets

One little tadpole came out of his spawn
It was a miracle when it happened at dawn
Was very small for those first few days
But all of Class 8 were shouting hoorays
Then they got out and made us all smile
They carried on for quite a while
Then they evolved to have front legs
This happened when our coats were on pegs
Now they are close to becoming frogs
They soon shall e found in muddy bogs.

Katherine Bradley (9)
Gardners Lane Primary School, Cheltenham

Lola The Dog

Lola is my pet dog,
I watch her lie on a log!

One day, she was fast asleep,
But when you make a sound, she will leap!

Her big, fluffy, fat tail
Is so big like a whale!

She is very lazy,
She never smells like a daisy!

When you stroke her hair,
She runs upstairs.

You will want to keep this lovely pup,
When you see her, you will want to get up.

Ruby Harper (9)
Gardners Lane Primary School, Cheltenham

A Peculiar Squirrel

A strange animal gliding through the sky
Is a squirrel.
Very questionable sight,
Washing up the dirty cutlery by licking it clean!
Very interesting doing the laundry,
Instead of putting the washing in...
He front-flipped in the machine.
Doing the housework,
But also making it worse.
He runs a bubbly bath...
Oops! He flooded the bathroom,
Now he has more work to do.

Gracie Slee (10)
Gardners Lane Primary School, Cheltenham

The Cat Who Makes His Own Breakfast!

Walking downstairs to the kitchen
Putting the kettle on, time for tea

Do not forget the toast, yippee!
Get on the butter and the jam

Going back upstairs to the toilet
Waiting for the tea and toast

When he hears breakfast is ready
Rushing downstairs he goes

Carefully grabbing a tray so nobody awakes
Into his bed, eating and watching cat TV!

Hannah Clarke (10)
Gardners Lane Primary School, Cheltenham

Peculiar Pets

I have a pet hedgehog
Who likes to go every morning for a jog.

He takes his friends out for lunch,
But is not keen on brunch.

My hedgehog likes to sleep in the dark
When he finds the right place in the park.

Jimmy has lots of shiny spikes
And likes to go on long hikes.

A hedgehog is a lovely friend
And always stands up for you in the end.

Sam Montague (9)
Gardners Lane Primary School, Cheltenham

A Peculiar Squirrel

My squirrel likes to drive
In my dad's favourite car.

It likes to do the washing-up,
Likes to cook for all of us.

He likes to sleep in my shoes
And snores like a dog dead asleep.

It's always in our pool, sunbathing,
We can't believe this is happening.

At night, he reads to us
His favourite book - 'Jack and the Beanstalk'.

Harry Dawson (10)
Gardners Lane Primary School, Cheltenham

Super Puppy

My puppy has a secret power
Can you guess?

She can fly like a superhero
Sometimes I mistake her for a superhero!

She barks and her cage deploys
Ad her mask is strapped on!

She saved people whilst flying
And lands gracefully

Is it a bird?
A plane?
No! It's Super Pup!

She really is a peculiar pet!

Evie Davis (10)
Gardners Lane Primary School, Cheltenham

Tommy The Raccoon

I have a pet that is a big fluffy raccoon,
Tommy likes to sleep in his small rough cocoon.

His stomach is big and white,
But be careful, he might hug you too tight.

My pet Tommy can sometimes smell,
So be warned as he waits in a well.

He won't move, he will fart and is lazy,
So cover your nose, as he will not smell like a daisy.

Jasmine Loveridge (10)
Gardners Lane Primary School, Cheltenham

The Bald Eagle

Jerry is my pet bald eagle,
Some say he squawks like a seagull.

One day, he lost a feather,
We were out in bad weather.

His head is white like a snowy kite,
His wings are brown like a dirty crown.

Jerry likes to dance
With a lot of romance.

When you see Jerry fly,
He will give a big wave goodbye.

Nacho Comeche Tallester (10)
Gardners Lane Primary School, Cheltenham

The Silly Seal

I have a pet seal that likes to steal
Which I think is very illegal
He's always been of great appeal
For a deal

He likes the colour teal
Always will reach for his meal.
He's lazy
And won't smell like a daisy.

Sammy will be your friend for real.
His tail is silky
Like it, it is milky.

Ayo Gabriel (10)
Gardners Lane Primary School, Cheltenham

Parmer The Amazing Llama

L ying lazily, watching TV.
L ikes to eat tacos with his friends.
A stonishing amount of saves as a superhero.
M aking portals with his unpleasant spit.
A mazing at teleporting the ball to the goal.

Astounding facts about Parmer.
Parmer has only tacos at parties with his friends.

Bobby Locke (10)
Gardners Lane Primary School, Cheltenham

Sparky

S parky always sings lullabies to the baby sister of mine
P ays £10 to me as I help him
A happy evening because he cooked sausage and mash
R emembers to wash the dishes always
K aty is a cat friend of Sparky's
Y ells out loud, "Storytime only for an hour!"

Mason Mchugh (10)
Gardners Lane Primary School, Cheltenham

Doctor Llama Strange

- **L** ikes chilling in his pyjamas, watching Netflix.
- **L** oves completing his crosswords after dinner.
- **A** dores eating his tacos - always spilling some on his pyjamas.
- **M** agnificent at skydiving - as she always does every Thursday.
- **A** nswering the door, somehow speaking English.

James Hollaway (9)
Gardners Lane Primary School, Cheltenham

Doctor Llama

My llama is a special one
That works really hard
But sometimes she is a magician
That fakes her tactics
She eats tacos
While riding her scooter down the road
My llama is a doctor too!
But she is always dancing
Twisting, swirling like a cloud
Upon her dainty feet.

Diego Milena (9)
Gardners Lane Primary School, Cheltenham

The Stinking Skunk

My pet skunk
Was sitting on a bunk,
Tipping all his junk
What a punk!

Riley is my skunk's name,
He has a deadly aim

He always wears a little hat
Sometimes I give him a pat.

My pet likes to dance
He even won a competition in France.

Ruby Didcote (10)
Gardners Lane Primary School, Cheltenham

The King Over All Cobras

King Cobra is my pet,
He once bit a vet.

If the king cobra smells something fresh,
He will strike if it is sweet flesh.

I took my friend for lunch
And my pet had a lovely crunch.

Jeffry loves to have a bite of you
So please stay away, I beg you.

Tyler-James Finn (10)
Gardners Lane Primary School, Cheltenham

Sunny The Dog

"My name is Sunny,
I am a blue puppy

I am a small fluffy dog,
Lying on a really tiny log.

I hate to job
Because I'm a dog."

She is cute and fun
And she likes the sun

Dogs love logs,
But they don't like fog.

Shelby Collins Chambers (9)
Gardners Lane Primary School, Cheltenham

David And Me

I have a blue dog
Who can sit on a log.

He is called David and he is cool,
I wish I could take him to school.

He has a bed,
It is really cute with his ted.

David is the best ever dog,
Maybe he needs a friend like a big pet hog.

Archie Orpin (9)
Gardners Lane Primary School, Cheltenham

My Dancing Dog

My dancing dog
Can Samba on a log.

Her name is Annabell,
She doesn't smell.

She tap-dances in the park,
But not if it's after dark.

Annabell spins like a top,
But when she gets started, she can't stop.

Layla-Rose Dorling (9)
Gardners Lane Primary School, Cheltenham

Casper The Cute, Fluffy Puppy

I have a puppy,
He is very funny.

He loves to roll on his tummy,
It is really soft and fluffy.

His smooth soft tail
Has fur like what comes off a bale.

Casper is my puppy's name,
He can fly a plane.

Maisie Hester (10)
Gardners Lane Primary School, Cheltenham

The Funny Bunny

The bunny is very funny,
He can jiggle with his fluffy tummy.

Daisy is his name,
Many say he has no game.

He has a tail
As big as a baby whale.

His hops can be big,
But not as big as a pig.

Oscar Lightstone (9)
Gardners Lane Primary School, Cheltenham

My Peculiar Pet

My character is a dog.
My dog is strange because he chews plastic.
My dog is unique because he isn't playing with his toys.
My dog is odd because he likes to lick my ear.
Sometimes my dog is sad and happy.

Jack Aguirre (10)
Gardners Lane Primary School, Cheltenham

My Peculiar Pet

My little bunny is so cute and funny,
She just rolls on her tiny fluffy tummy.
She sleeps on my pink top bunk,
She also loves hippity-hop, pop, punk and funk.

On weekdays, me and Miss Runny Babbit can only hop so far
Because on the weekends, she turns into a... pop star!

And when she hops on stage, the crowd sing, cheer and shout.
Miss Runny Babbit is what it's all about!
Some shed a tear in amazement and glee,
For she is so good and fabulous, you see.

After her marvellous gig, she goes home
To a mug of hot chocolate and to read a nice poem

And when it's the weekday, she is full of bounce and play.
Now we know her secret, we must not say!

Emily Hemphill (11)
Gillygooley Primary School, Omagh

My Peculiar Pet

Charlie the cow is my best friend.
Yes, he's a cow, but I might start a trend.
He sleeps in my bed and snores at night.
The bed isn't big enough but we just fight in right.
He eats my fluffy carpet because it is green,
He is the best mate I've ever seen!
Charlie the cow, my milk he likes to drink,
The only problem is he uses the sink.
I don't like it when he eats my dinner,
But at the local village market, he's always a winner.

Yes! My best friend might be a cow,
But I wouldn't change that, not even now!
If I'm upset, he's the first to come see,
If you find Charlie, you will always find me!

Jack Walker (10)
Gillygooley Primary School, Omagh

My Peculiar Pet

My pet, Cherry the cheetah,
She's fluffy, cute and I'd like you to meet her,
Cherry loves to run so fast,
When we race, it means I always come last.

Cherry loves to dance and sing,
She dances to her little song,
When I don't pass my test, she says, "You tried your best,"
When she plays with her toys, she always makes a big mess.

Even when she's naughty, I still love her forever,
When we were out walking, she met her friend Trevor,
She loves to go on walks to get some fresh air,
When I'm away at school, she loves to say her prayers.

Natasha Elliott (10)
Gillygooley Primary School, Omagh

My Peculiar Pet

Giraffey Giraffe, a rare species of giraffe,
Giraffey Giraffe sings in the bath,
Giraffey Giraffe, his neck so steep,
Giraffey Giraffe stands to sleep.

Giraffey Giraffe, big brown spots,
Giraffey Giraffe eats lots and lots,
Giraffey Giraffe eats the trees in my garden,
Giraffey Giraffe burps! Oh, beg your pardon.

Giraffey Giraffe escaped from the wild,
Giraffey Giraffe escaped as a child,
Giraffey Giraffe walked for miles as a calf,
Giraffey Giraffe's past is worth the laugh.

Zoey Crankshaw (11)
Gillygooley Primary School, Omagh

My Peculiar Pet

Sammy Sloth is super slow,
He loves his food but he doesn't grow
Cos when he bothers to stand up,
He's only the size of a little teacup.

His silky fur is striped, purple and green,
He's continuously careful to keep it clean,
On his head he has a bowler hat
And he loves to fly on his magical mat.

Although Sammy Sloth is super strange,
I really don't want him to change
Cos he's really friendly, fun and kind,
That is why I don't mind!

Rachel Nelson (11)
Gillygooley Primary School, Omagh

My Peculiar Pet

My pet cat is a fluffy boy
Who runs around with all his toys,
My neighbour said he makes too much noise,
But he is still my funny, fluffy boy.

But when it's time,
He'll go out and fight crime.

Bat Cat, oh Bat Cat, where are you?
There is a heist on North Avenue,
Don't let that man take all the food,
Bat Cat, Bat Cat, oh where are you?
Bat Cat, Bat Cat, there you are!
Stop that robber right this time
And make sure he gets a massive fine.

Harry McCormack (11)
Gillygooley Primary School, Omagh

My Peculiar Pet

I have a pet hippo, he always drinks my juice,
Then sometimes he thinks he's a moose
When we go to the park,
We will always find a dog that will bark.

He once went with me to school,
But he fell into a pool,
Going home, he enjoyed the school bus
But then all the children made a fuss.

I love my pet hippo, he is really nice,
He is even good at scaring away the mice.

Mark Cousins (11)
Gillygooley Primary School, Omagh

My Peculiar Pet

M y pet gorilla is called Gerry
Y es, a pet gorilla so tiny like a cherry.

G erry is so very scary.
O verall, Gerry is my best berry.
R eally, Gerry has a girlfriend called Mary.
I n the cold, he is always merry.
L ove him when he is hairy like a teddy.
L ike him even if you're weary.
A lways love him and Mary.

Emily Mackey (10)
Gillygooley Primary School, Omagh

Miss Molly Mouse

My pet's name is Miss Molly Mouse McSqueak!
She has been working at Cheesy Restaurant for one week
Yesterday, she spilt all the soup
But Molly cleaned it up with help from the rest of the troop
Sometimes she brings her cheese-shaped teddy
And she loves her hat called Eddie
Molly's tail is fourteen miles long!
On the end of it there's a bell. *Ding-dong!*
She likes to be alone
But she hugs me at home
Molly snuggled me on my shoulder
I hope she stays with me until I'm older.

Amelie Seymour (10)
Guilden Morden CE Primary Academy, Guilden Morden

About Sharpedo

S cary shark lives in my bottomless pond
H e likes to eat raw salmon from the shops
A nd his tricks include jumping out of my pond and back in again
R ules do not matter to him, so he is a rule breaker
P eople are very scared of him because he is ferocious.
E ven when he's asleep, he's still scary.
D iving under the water and eating the fish in my pond
O pen mouth, ready to eat you.

Freddie Barnes (8)
Guilden Morden CE Primary Academy, Guilden Morden

Cautious The Chameleon

C ome and try to see my colourful chameleon
H e is playful and good at hide-and-seek
A spy, he is amazing and he is spectacular
M onsters don't scare him
E h, he does not know his maths
L ove his owner, which is me
E nergetic is his middle name
O n a tree and a mighty one at that
N ever a dull day for me.

Harrison Catheart (8)
Guilden Morden CE Primary Academy, Guilden Morden

Kily The Kitzune

Kily the Kitzune was rushing through the enchanted wood,
she had to get to her shop that sells lovely hoods.
Her fur was shining blue and pink,
and you'll miss her if you blink.
All the other creatures in the enchanted wood,
go to her shop because it is so good,
and if you go deep,
into that forest,
you'll find her cottage, called Good Greens Crest.

Esther Cutler (8)
Guilden Morden CE Primary Academy, Guilden Morden

Sally Squirrel

S uper cheeky
A nd loves nuts
L ittle but fierce
L ong white teeth
Y ellow face

S ally is cute
Q ueen of the thief
U ses a crown
I know she's cute but she's bad too
R ummaging
R eally hungry
E very day hunts for nuts
L oves to steal.

Ophelia Hall (8)
Guilden Morden CE Primary Academy, Guilden Morden

Super Dog

As Super Dog ran like a frog
And he saw a hedgehog
He was thinking to rob a bank
And thought he would become first rank
When he saw the president
Super Dog said, "I'm a UK resident."
He was jailed because his plan had failed
As he said to himself, "Super Dog is no more,"
And listened to his mother snore.

Daniel Taran (9)
Guilden Morden CE Primary Academy, Guilden Morden

Westen The Whale

Westen the whale was very shy
He swam in the sea as the people waved by
Westen went down and found a clown
Down in the deep, Westen took a peep
There was a seahorse ready to have more force
Ready to make a fight but not too tight!

Bethany Maley (11)
Guilden Morden CE Primary Academy, Guilden Morden

The Cat Poem

Ginger the cat is very smart and clever.
She doesn't like the dark, never, never, never!
In the daytime, with her cape,
She likes to play, fly and eat grapes
And likes to dance in the rain
And doesn't get any pain.

Ella-Louise Groom (9)
Guilden Morden CE Primary Academy, Guilden Morden

Fiery Tails

I have a nine tails locked inside my body
Asleep for a very long time
That gives me ultimate powers of sun
He comes out mostly to fight
With gigantic tails that can destroy hotels
But he is even stronger with me.

Andrew Speed (11)
Guilden Morden CE Primary Academy, Guilden Morden

The Sloppy Sloth

Sloppy the sloth on the tree
What could happen? Nothing, surely
A woodpecker comes, picks my tree
Then it crumbles all over me
I go to find some friends to help
No one in sight, I am all by myself...

Devon Julyan1 (11)
Guilden Morden CE Primary Academy, Guilden Morden

The Flying TNT Dog

Boom, boom, boom
A dog is in town
He blows up and
Flies like an eagle

Woof, woof, woof
He's a normal dog in the day
He is the best dog ever.

Boom, boom, boom
He flies in shining white moonlight
I look out my window

Woof, woof, woof
I grow wings
I play with my dog like a pro
When I'm there, he's there

Boom, boom, boom
This is my song
Hope you enjoy
When I and my dog fly away.

Fernando Alondia Almeida-Amos (9)
Halewood CE Primary School, Halewood

Looie The Lion

As bombs rained on London Zoo
My friend Looie was asleep, *ah-shoo*
He lay in the corner of his cage

As I called his name
I grasped the key
Unlocked the cage and ran through Park Lane

Past the penguins, pandas and parrots
I clambered on his back
We waved goodbye to London Zoo

All the animals were scared and blue
Gunshots all around
My heart started to pound

He unusually liked this sound
Smoke filled the air
But Looie kept going

All night long
We travelled until Big Ben went *bong!*
It was time to go home

I got in bed
Looie on the end
And whispered, "Goodnight."

My peculiar pet!

Sienna Mutch (9)
Halewood CE Primary School, Halewood

Lucie Flies

Lucie the panda is special to me
She loves eating bark off a tree
She is very special to me
So I let her be what she wants to be

Lucie is neon in the night
As she takes flight
She hates the dark
But she loves tree bark

So she always takes a light
Before she takes flight
When she flies
She soars up into the skies

Sometimes she takes me
So I can see what she wants to be
She is very furry like a bunny
And she is soo funny

I can see what she wants to be
When she takes me
She wants to be a pandacorn
When her babies are born.

Lucie Moss (9)
Halewood CE Primary School, Halewood

Silly Songs Poem

Hippo: Hi, I'm Sarah,
I like to eat your burger,
When you say my name
I will say, "Sheeran."

Cat: Hi, I'm Claire
I like to eat your hair
When you say my name
I will shout, "Champagne!"

Gorilla: Hi, I'm Mary
I am very, very scary.
When you say my name
I will eat your brain!

Zebra: Hi, I'm Snipy
I'm very stripy,
When you say my name
I have your vein.

Monkey: Hi, I'm Kelly
My mother's very smelly.

When you say my name
I will put you in pain.

Ella-Sofia Hennity (9)
Halewood CE Primary School, Halewood

Peculiar Pet

I am a dog, a lion and a hare
Also a pig, cat and a bear
And you can call me whatever you wish
I also enjoy a dish of fish.
I know you will like me if you're a child
Because I always like to run wild.

I am kind, friendly and sweet
Even though I do eat meat
I also enjoy playing fetch the ball
In the great, grand, big hall.
The great, grand hall is a place
I like to make a disgrace.

Now it is time for me to say goodbye
So I can have my tea.

Kaitlin Potts (9)
Halewood CE Primary School, Halewood

Fodwing

Fodwing has a strange mind
And he's the only one of his kind
He loves to fly all day

His name is Cat Fish but call him Flame
He doesn't like his real name
And he thinks flies are delicious

He roars like a lion
And sprays water out of his trunk
He thinks he's a real punk

He talks like a human
He is as cute as a kitten
And wears Louis Vitton

He is very feisty
His favourite food is fish
He always has a wish.

Sophie Lloyd (9)
Halewood CE Primary School, Halewood

Trevor

The courageous young Komodo flies
He flaps his wings and cries.
He is very brave and clever
He likes to be called Trevor.

He wobbles his googly eyes
And doesn't like goodbyes
He will bite
It's not a pleasant sight

He's two metres wide
He walks with some pride
You don't want to stroke him
His skin is very grim

He may not be speedy
But his eyes are very beady
He uses his venom
And wears double denim.

Samuel Rooney (9)
Halewood CE Primary School, Halewood

The Spy Cat

The Spy Cat doesn't sit on a mat
She doesn't chase a rat
And no, she doesn't wear a hat

She doesn't catch a frog
And she doesn't scratch a log
Or jump in a bog

She fights crime
Retrieves a dime
And investigates an abandoned mine

She jumps in the air
Saves a school fair
and finds a criminal's lair.

You've heard of Spy Cat
Who doesn't wear a hat
Or sit on a mat.

Ava Stephens (8)
Halewood CE Primary School, Halewood

Shamingo's Daily Life!

Haiku poetry

The sass bird alert,
Always in a perfect mood,
A clumsy spirit.

Never had a crush,
With her feathery pink skin,
She makes the boys blush.

She likes eating fish,
It has to be nice and fresh,
It's her favourite dish.

She enjoys singing,
Actually, it's her dream,
It's like bells ringing.

The end of the day,
It's time to go to sleep now,
The animals lie.

Annie Williams (9)
Halewood CE Primary School, Halewood

King Lioncoon

Oh look, there is a lion lurking
All around its cage
He scares his peers
Leaving them in tears
He has a big cheeky grin
Saying, "I will only be a minute."
His eyes are bright red
And he has his own bed
His teeth are razor-sharp
If he bites you, it will leave a mark
He's met Clark Kent
He is a torment
He's two metres wide
And walks in pride
He's a peculiar pet.

Elise McGregor (9)
Halewood CE Primary School, Halewood

Kittycorn

K ate the Kittycorn is very special
I ncredible in the night when she takes flight
T he dark does not scare her
T he dark is actually a friend of hers
Y es, it is incredible, she does not take lessons
C an she do loop-de-loops in the sky
O r would she prefer to glide?
R epeating moves all night long
N ext time she will take me along.

Sophie Dean (8)
Halewood CE Primary School, Halewood

My Peculiar Pet

Every day, I go on a walk
With my dog called Pola
He's a big fat dog and he looks short
He's an ordinary dog
Just different by the size

He gets called fat
But he fights back when he gets bullied
He calls them a bully

I'm so lucky to have him
He's the saviour of everyone
He can fight whatever animal
If he loses, he doesn't give up.

Joshua Healey (9)
Halewood CE Primary School, Halewood

My Pet Fred

My pet Fred
Loves to go to bed
My pet Fred jumps around in joy
When he found one, he had a friend called Roy

My pet Fred loves to eat
But when it comes to tests, he loves to cheat
My pet Fred wants to go in a pool
But my pet Fred is in school

My pet Fred has crazy hair
Everybody stops to stare
My pet Fred needs to rest
He always tries his best.

Daniel Fitzsimmons (8)
Halewood CE Primary School, Halewood

Screaming Al

Screaming Al bakes cakes
Flies like a pigeon but as dirty as a pig
Loves to eat bakes.

Always daydreaming
But flying is his thing
The moonlight shines on him.

Running after bees
That's exercise done for now
Time for another sleep.

Running on the floor
Screaming Al is all but love
My peculiar pet.

Ellie McGregor (9)
Halewood CE Primary School, Halewood

Marvellous Dog

Every day I go for a flight
Every day my amazing owner is polite
Every day my wings come up
I have a friend called Pup

I am called Marvellous Dog
Yesterday I ate a frog
I am very sassy
My best friend is called Cassy

I am clever
I have to wear leather
If I were alone, I would never.

Daniel Glover (8)
Halewood CE Primary School, Halewood

The Racing Giraffe

Haiku poetry

The Racing Giraffe
It can out-sprint anything
It's unbeatable

Nothing is faster
Not even a fast cheetah
Who would like a race?

Everyone is scared
Should be in the Olympics
It would win easy

Would be the best pet
It is so adorable
It is fully trained.

Ethan Wells (9)
Halewood CE Primary School, Halewood

Pek, Pek

My spy chick is cute
He has a suit
He is tiny
But his sunglasses are really shiny

He is the boss
If you get fired, it is your loss
He is very clever
And he has a jacket made from leather

He is furry
But sometimes scary
He is not lazy
And he has a friend Daisy.

Mae Anders (9)
Halewood CE Primary School, Halewood

My Fun Phoenix

A blazing phoenix
Is my peculiar pet,
It squawks and it hawks.

A blazing strong beast,
A scorching fire bird,
A mythical sight.

It spits out fire,
Shrieking and shining,
When rising higher

Goddess of fire
Her name is the Mighty Blitz
A fire spirit.

Isla Fearns (9)
Halewood CE Primary School, Halewood

TNT Chicken

TNT Chicken
He loves to buy TNT
He is dangerous

Like an asteroid
Hitting the Earth as fast as
A leopard chasing

He looks like a bomb
When he is angry or mad
He will blow up

He is my bomb pet
That looks like a chicken pet
That blows up like a bomb.

Oliver Banlin (9)
Halewood CE Primary School, Halewood

The Great Dog (Tom)

My pet is Tom
It's intelligent
It really likes books

It's a fun dog
It likes to talk about books
Really weird books

It likes to walk
And tummy tickles
He is no danger

Feel free to stroke
Don't feed him diet Coke
He is a good boy.

Jake Cardwell (9)
Halewood CE Primary School, Halewood

Cyber-Dog

Secret spy from a mad future
Where robots roam the whole world
Cyber-Dog has come!

He roams around the city
Cheers across his whole home
Protecting the weak.

He is amazing
Even faster than a cheetah
As strong as an ox.

Herbie T Webb (8)
Halewood CE Primary School, Halewood

All About Smurfles

Smurfles, who wants to be a cat,
He has a funky hat
And he can't use a bat.

He wears his sports clothes,
he doesn't like the hairbows
but nobody knows.

He is cute
not too minute
but bigger than a newt.

Charlie Walker (9)
Halewood CE Primary School, Halewood

The Rocking Horse Of Midnight

I got a rocking horse when I was three,
I felt splendid, overjoyed and filled with glee,
I named her Gwen, the best name ever,
I knew I would keep her lovingly forever.
One night, I woke up and saw her disappear!
Another night, I crept out and followed her here.
Where? You may ask. Into the night sky, of course!
She just turned into a fully grown horse!
Extraordinary wings and long eyelashes brushing her fur,
I rode on her back until we were tired,
We soared through the sky, soared until we were tired.
Gwen is fierce, certainly number one
And our little secret is great and fun!

Kalina Walczak (9)
Larchfield Primary & Nursery School, Maidenhead

Wonder Pet Subahstyck

S ubahstyck can transform into the animals he is made of.
U nbelievably, he is a mixture of a cat, dog, bunny and a fish.
B ubbles come out of his mouth if he is happy.
A kind emotion is always inside him.
H e runs super speedily to escape from danger.
S ausages are his favourite food.
T o flop on his back is as soft as a sack.
Y ou can touch a part of his body, he will become what you touched.
C oughing and sneezing, Subahstyck is here, he heals you with pleasure, hooray!
K ind is what is the best.

Polina Nahimovics (8)
Larchfield Primary & Nursery School, Maidenhead

Kodog, My Pet

Kodog is my pet, I found him at the pound.
Nobody wanted him, he was a funny little greyhound.
I took pity on him, but the shopkeeper told me that it was part koala
And that it wasn't a boy, it was a girl, and her name was Tala.
I picked her up and paid at the till,
I was about to exit when she told me Tala could fly
Really high in the sky
And change colour to the scarf I was wearing around my neck.
She also said that Tala could teleport wherever I desire,
Even into a fire.
From that day,
We used to play,
She is a good pet every day.

Emma Pennington (8)
Larchfield Primary & Nursery School, Maidenhead

The Best Pet Ever, Starfires

S tarfires has a tail that's as long as a 100m wire
T he best pet ever, she is definitely clever
A red furry collar, her second-best friend is Mrs Mollar
R eady for dinner, she is always a winner
F ire on her arms and head, always sleeps in her cosy bed
I love her beautiful humps on her back, also she loves to chat
R eally loves her nuts, not her gloves
E merald-green eyes as shiny as the sun
S uch a beautiful tail with lots of colours.

Imaad Rahman (9)
Larchfield Primary & Nursery School, Maidenhead

Sassy Dass Daily Routine

Sassy Dass thinks she's the best of the rest,
She has fiery wings that no one has yet.
She's not that honey bunny, more like money bunny.
She can fly away up high in that night sky.
But when I want a ride, she never goes high
Only a few seconds and she's done.
She knows her stuff, she's number one at all times.
In the night, she's asleep
I am not having a peek.
I need some sleep for me.
I am not ready for another day like this painful day.

Sabeeha Shahzad (9)
Larchfield Primary & Nursery School, Maidenhead

Dogicorn

D ogicorn likes purple chocolate and her red hair shines
O h so bright, and takes off for flight
G orgeous like a starry night, in the day so rude to me too
I n the day, she sends people to the dogicorn master
C oming through the sky, oh so angry as a bear
O h, be scared when you look at her, she will make your day
R unning low on energy
N ow or never, need to hide from the two, best team ever!

Sophie Horwood (9)
Larchfield Primary & Nursery School, Maidenhead

Crabicorn's Life!

C rabicorn is always being the boss,
R ushing her work while eating moss,
A lways sitting on the sand while being lazy
B ecause of her attitude, she flies away like crazy
I nside her room, I see holes in the wall,
C hoking on food all day long while haunting the halls,
O n top of shelves, pooping furry gum
R unning around with a drum
N ow she nearly bashed into the wall.

Alexia Pascu (9)
Larchfield Primary & Nursery School, Maidenhead

Rude Dog Fly

R ude Dog Fly
U nexpectedly ruder than my other pet
D own he goes with his weak wings
E asy to maintain, the best pet in the world

D eer or dog, you name it
O ranges are his favourite food
G rowls like a bear, sleeps like a cat

F lies with other butterflies
L oves red more than anyone
Y ou will not believe what he has done.

Diya Thumsi (8)
Larchfield Primary & Nursery School, Maidenhead

Pandahorn

P andahorn is the best, better than the rest.
A pples are her favourite food, she is always in a mood.
N ever be mean, Pandahorn is the best to be seen.
D on't mess with her, she can be bossy.
A dorable she is and loyal too.
H ates people except me.
O nly likes to fly, never walks.
R ain is her favourite
N ight sky, she turns into a doll.

Julia Miklas (9)
Larchfield Primary & Nursery School, Maidenhead

Pandacorn

P andacorn is the best, better than the rest
A pples are her treat
N icest pet you'll ever meet
D on't mess with her, she might curse you
A ll animals are her friends
C olour pink is her first favourite colour
O h, you will never forget meeting her
R ainbow clothes are her favourite
N ot even harmful, she is one nice pet.

Rakshitha Ramesh-Babu (8)
Larchfield Primary & Nursery School, Maidenhead

Pangrill

P angrill likes to eat but not luxury meat.
A banana and bamboo is her favourite food.
N obody comes near her because she is oh so scary.
G orgeous like a starry night sky.
R eally lazy and she's super crazy.
I 'm so happy that she can teleport.
L oads of huge rocks and trees to build a house.
L ovely and as kind as could be.

Starla Saw (8)
Larchfield Primary & Nursery School, Maidenhead

Marshakune

M y favourite snack is marshmallow
A ll I do is go to the meadows
R eally eager fairies, vermillion hair
S ome days I stay up to watch the sunset till dark
H appy me, happy everybody
A lways you will make friends
K angaroos are my friends
U nicorns don't like kangaroos
N ot a fan of day
E njoy night.

Breah Rance (9)
Larchfield Primary & Nursery School, Maidenhead

Scullsnake

S hiny, sharp, protruded teeth
C rawls and creeps in the night
U p all night and sleeps all day
L ikes to climb up trees
L ooks like a skeleton
S coring points when playing games
N eeds to be fed four times a day
A cts like a python
K ind to everyone he meets
E specially me!

Tyler Brench (9)
Larchfield Primary & Nursery School, Maidenhead

Crocodog

C rocodog is eating fish.
R ivers have lots of fish.
O ver there, she is swimming slowly.
C rocodog has scales, no fur.
O range fish swim around her.
D oes she sneeze out of her dog nose?
O r does she chomp the branches?
G oing in the water, saying, "Hello, fish."

Nithila Suganthan (9)
Larchfield Primary & Nursery School, Maidenhead

My Pet

P egdog is the best, friendly in any way
E very day after school, I get on her back, she takes me in a flash.
G oes to Misty Meadows, flies home in a flash
D reamy-coloured wings, furry strong back
O n her mattress she sleeps, then snores, then a small peep.
G ives the best warm hugs.

Falisha Khan (8)
Larchfield Primary & Nursery School, Maidenhead

Dastardly

Dastardly is sneaking and peeking everywhere you go
And don't forget he has tiny feet.
So stay at home.
Dastardly is very sneaky
And don't be scared, he is not a bear
Wriggling out of the wood
Don't forget to wake up at dawn, then you'll yawn
Lazy all the time
You don't cry.

Jayme Figueira (9)
Larchfield Primary & Nursery School, Maidenhead

Unidog

Unidog is the best, better than the rest.
His wings shine so bright in the light.
He is the best dog, he can see through fog.
Me and him love to race to space.
He can fly to the sky.
His tail can splash like a whale.
He will be clever forever and has a unicorn horn,
Cute eyes and never lies.

Freddie Branch (9)
Larchfield Primary & Nursery School, Maidenhead

Bunnyfly's World

B unnyflies fly all around
U sually like to swing on the swing
N ow they are at the park
N ever played on the park
Y oghurt makes them jump
F lowers are their favourite plant
L oud as a panda
Y ou will see them everywhere.

Anaiza Fernandez (9)
Larchfield Primary & Nursery School, Maidenhead

Unirump

U ni loves playing hide-and-seek
N aughty, every day saying bye to people
I t entertains me every day
R iding her I love to do
U nirump has so much fun with me
M ood is happy every day
P eople scare her every day, I make her happy.

Jessie Savage (9)
Larchfield Primary & Nursery School, Maidenhead

The Dactus

D og, cat? Oh, what's that?
A Dactus! Look at his cactus tail.
C actus pricked, don't pet this tail.
T o feed it, give it golden cookies.
U p high in the sky, it likes to sleep,
S o be careful in the open, it might bite!

Marina Kemp-Brown (9)
Larchfield Primary & Nursery School, Maidenhead

Crampy

C rampy is always cranky, every day he is angry
R eally colourful and furry
A ll I do is camouflage all day with him
M y favourite food is bones.
P arty games are his favourite games
Y ou might be confused but it's cool.

Anthony Duffy (9)
Larchfield Primary & Nursery School, Maidenhead

Go Catcorn

Glows like a light, shines so bright
Oval face like an egg, calls like an owl
Crawls like a cow
All its body is covered in fur
Cold like ice
Quiet like mice
Oh yeah, go Catcorn races like a car
So far
No one can hurt her.

Layla Clarke (8)
Larchfield Primary & Nursery School, Maidenhead

Unipig

U nipig is always tame.
N o one likes seeing her grumpy.
I always see her being cheeky.
P ink is her favourite colour.
I ncredibly bossy.
G oing near is not a good idea.

Holly Jones (9)
Larchfield Primary & Nursery School, Maidenhead

Fogs

The Fog's bed is enormous
Its favourite treat is a golden treat
It completes legendary quests
They live in the jungle in a doggy treat palace
In their house are tubes that take them to different dimensions.

Andrew Gillespie (9)
Larchfield Primary & Nursery School, Maidenhead

Henry The Goatydog

H enry the Goatydog was outside
E ating an apple, he was also eating a chicken
"N o, no, no!" said his mum, Mrs Goatydog
R ory, his dad, came outside and said
"Y ou Goat... come in now!"

G oatydog was sad, he shouldn't have eaten the chicken
O lly came through his bedroom window. "Hi friend," said Olly
"A ll the chicken in the world is so yummy," said Goatydog
"T hat is true," said Olly, "but it's only chicken
Y our mum and dad are crazy! Why
D o your mum and dad hate you eating chicken?"
"O h! I don't know why, it's just weird." "Well, I have to go, bye"
G oatydog said bye too.

Cameron Clifford (8)
Lochnell Primary School, Benderloch

Slimey The Shark

Slimey, oh Slimey, oh Slimey the shark
What joy it brings me to watch you play
You may be as big as a panda bear
But I don't care!
You are, and always will be my favourite pet
I feed you twice a day
I try to get out of your way
Although it is a challenge
A good challenge indeed
Because I get your love, of course
Oh Slimey, oh Slimey, oh Slimey the shark
When I get a new fish, I hear you say...
"The only one who should be here is me!"
I leave for a second and come back
And to my surprise, you are twice the size!
Poor fish indeed!
Oh Slimey, oh Slimey, oh Slimey the shark,
You will always be my favourite
Forever the love will grow.

Calum Kill (9)
Lochnell Primary School, Benderloch

Tilly The Saber-Tooth Frilled Crab-Bat

Tilly is gentle, Tilly is tame
Tilly is lazy, Tilly is scaled.

Tilly's wings are blue, feathery and fluffy
Her scales are hard just like a roughy

She is lime-green, purple and dark blue
And be careful, she might bite you!

Sometimes she can be clever and quick
Her slim body is agile and slick!

The spikes on her back are actually teeth!
She has claws like a crab from a coral reef.

A frill around her neck like a Christmas wreath
And zigzags on her stomach underneath.

She might be grumpy, messy and lazy
But under it all, she's still Tilly.

Eachan MacDonald (8)
Lochnell Primary School, Benderloch

The Treacherous Tulla

The treachery of her eyes
Burning a dark bronze
She sees someone
She opens her mouth and... yawns
She barks a terrific bark
It echoes around the world
She knocks the door down
And blasts a laser from her yawning mouth
She walks to the top of the cliff
Her black and white coat blows in the wind
Like a lion after winning a battle
She walks to the end of the cliff and has a sniff
She said to herself, "I'm sniffing some tiffin!"
Off she goes, off the cliff!

Lewis Hart (10)
Lochnell Primary School, Benderloch

The Cute Wolf-Unicorn-Fly

Fluffy and Duffy were playing in the woods
Then they saw a little girl reading a book
When she noticed them
She asked if she could ride on their backs
So they let her get on their back
They laid down and she hopped on
As they were running she held onto their neck
When they stopped running, she said
"I have to go now, my dad is looking for me"
So they took her back
She hugged them and said bye
They never knew you could have a girl as a pet!

Mirren MacDonald (10)
Lochnell Primary School, Benderloch

The Wacky Wollie

T errific and true
H appy and hooting
E verlasting fun

W hooping and wallowing
A n amazing acrobat
C lever and cool
K raken is crazy, but...
Y ou know that it is never as crazy as her!

W ow! Watch her go!
O h my, it's her!
L aughing and
L oving
I t is a cross between a Collie and a Whippet!
E xciting and extraordinary.

Sam Wilson (9)
Lochnell Primary School, Benderloch

Animal Adventures

J umping Gerald jumps his way
E ars up, ready to play
R umbles and tumbles
B leats for food
I ncluding Tim, with a friend
D inner is done, play is over
A nd goes to bed with a rumble in his tum

J aney tries to neigh, does not work
A mazed me with a headshake
N odding at herself
N eigh so loud
E ating happily
A nd says, "Yay!"

Grace Stewart (10)
Lochnell Primary School, Benderloch

Stick Insect

S uper stealthy stick insect
T hinking he would be best
I n the race
C rooked legs and shiny leaves
K im, his friend, got an award

I nside his treehouse
N ever sits down, always jumpy
S its down finally, then gets up and bounds
E very time he does this
C risps is what he loves
T his is what I have to deal with, so I trapped him in a box.

Angus Carswell (10)
Lochnell Primary School, Benderloch

My Peculier Pet

He's a giant snail
And he only comes out in the hail
He's a rabbit, duck, human, cat
He mostly eats leaves
Which really makes me queasy
He's really funny
When he wriggles his tummy
When I go to school
He plays in my pool
When I go to bed, I always dread...
He'll eat all the bread
When I wake up, he eats all my sister's make-up!
Which makes my brother wake up!

Skyela Stuart (9)
Lochnell Primary School, Benderloch

Quick, Quick!

Quick, quick!
We need to put the dinner on.
Quick, quick!
We need to feed the doghamster.
Quick, quick!
We need to go to the shopping mall.
Quick, quick!
We need to go home and get the dinner out.
Phew! That was close
He would have gobbled us up!
The doghamster is as wide as a dog
And as small as a hamster
A bit scary and it can change size...

Joshua MacNiven (9)
Lochnell Primary School, Benderloch

Pot Noodles

My fish likes noodles, Pot Noodles
He's very cool 'cause he doodles
He has a clan
And a plan
And that's why he's called Noodles
He likes to sing
His alarm goes *ding! Ding!*
Everyone comes to his door
He is not poor
He knows everything
He's lazy
And crazy
He's wild
Not mild
His memory is hazy.

Roan Waslidge (10)
Lochnell Primary School, Benderloch

My Pet, The Transformer Frog

A big frog, a pig frog
Cap frog, licking frog
Invisible frog, sappy nappy frog
Delightful frog, oh frog
Lovely frog, flying frog
An ugly frog, atomic bomb frog
Zapper frog, tall frog
Every guy, little frog
Rubbish frog, inflatable frog
Dump frog, kind frog
Eagle frog, elephant frog
Yummy frog, dead frog
Everlasting frog, robbed frog.

Dean Cotton (10)
Lochnell Primary School, Benderloch

The Shadow Horse

The black horse ran free
A shadow in the moonlight
Never to be seen
Galloping faster
Faster than a meteor
A single shadow
Tearing the ground up
Finally finding a cave
Tonight she is safe
The wind whistled desperately
She lays down carefully
The only glow, the moonlight
Shining like a spotlight
Tonight she sleeps peacefully.

Rosie Campbell (10)
Lochnell Primary School, Benderloch

The Doughnut Dog

The Doughnut is squishy and soft
He does not live in a loft
He's made of sugar and lives in the bakery hazily
He sleeps lazily
His favourite place to go is the croft

While at the croft
He got stuck in the loft
He did not know how to get out
He howled like a wolf but it sounded like a shout
He made a bed and it was super soft.

James Blomfield (11)
Lochnell Primary School, Benderloch

Harry The Dragocat

H arry can get
A ngry. Harry can be
R apid. Harry is
R esponsible. Harry is
Y outhful. Harry can be

D ramatic. Harry is
R ed. Harry is
A ctive. Harry is
G reat! Harry can be
O dd. Harry is
C razy. Harry can
A rgue. Harry is
T all.

Christopher MacLaurin (8)
Lochnell Primary School, Benderloch

Strange Creature, Strange

What a weird creature that lives in my house
Deadly but gentle, as scared as a mouse
It breathes fire and it likes to roar
Crawling about on the floor

Granny, pig and much more too
For an animal, it's too strange to be true
Tapping about with its centipede legs
Making a sound like scattering pegs.

Mac Rodwell (11)
Lochnell Primary School, Benderloch

Merret (Meerkat-Ferret)

M ini as can be, he flies across the city in the night sky
E ating a bit of cheese. I see him landing on the sign
R eading a bit, as his cheese goes in the breeze
R eading a bit more, I catch him to go to bed with me
E arly in the morning, I give him his egg and cheese and his
T ea!

Lucas Bonniwell (9)
Lochnell Primary School, Benderloch

Silly Lilly

I know a bat sugar glider named Lilly
Sometimes she is silly
She hangs upside down
She wears a nightgown
Her best friend is Billy

She fell out of the apple tree
Billy yelled, "Yippee!"
He helped her up
Then he got stung by a bee.

Caitlin MacColl (11)
Lochnell Primary School, Benderloch

Tiger

C unning, clever, caring
A mazing, awesome
T abby, tiger
S mart, stealthy

T errific
I ntelligent, ingenious
G reat
E xcellent, energetic, endangered
R apid
S pecial, super.

Thomas Davies
Lochnell Primary School, Benderloch

Moss
Haiku poetry

My dog is called Moss
He chases sheep for his job
Moss is always fun

He is black and white
He plays with his best friend, Fern
Spud does not like him

Rugby is his thing
He stares at the small lamb, Tim
I love him so much.

Alice Macdonald (10)
Lochnell Primary School, Benderloch

Frank The Fish

Frank lives in school
Students think he's cool
He is very lazy
Cause his vision is hazy
But he's not a fool

Frank leaves a mess
But he's not depressed
He is very cute
He likes to smell fruit
He is just the best.

James Steward (11)
Lochnell Primary School, Benderloch

Jim John

Tentacles and wings
Jim John, a messy monster
So crazy and wild

Some monsters, like Jim John
Are marvellous
But sometimes they are ferocious
They are messy and a little lazy
Also slimy
Don't forget the monster is dangerous!

Alasdair Bruce (10)
Lochnell Primary School, Benderloch

Fly

Flying high in the sky
A buzzy, fuzzy little fly
Above the clouds in the air
My little fly all covered in hair

Trying hard, my fly will be
Running away from a bee maybe
Getting food and flying home
Knowing that the bee is alone.

Lewis Shaw (11)
Lochnell Primary School, Benderloch

My Pet, Bob

Haiku poetry

My pet, Bob, is strange
He is a weird animal
He eats toast for tea

One day, my pet, Bob
Went on a walk in the park
He fell on some slime

I went to find him
I found him stuck in the slime
We went home again.

Alasdair Bullock (9)
Lochnell Primary School, Benderloch

The Loverlies

Don loves sums and sand and sun
And his fur is fluffy
He is so adorable
He is so cuddly
He is so sweet and kind
He is so special
He is kind and nice
He is super loud
He acts shy but is loud
I love Don.

Mia Travers (9)
Lochnell Primary School, Benderloch

My Pet, Sunshine

S o slimy
U nbearably messy
N ever wants a strawberry
S ometimes a banana
H ave an apple
I always want to play
N ectarines if I'm good
E xtraordinary.

Phoebe Lavis-Jones (9)
Lochnell Primary School, Benderloch

My Pet, Griffon

G riffon's eyes sparkle in the sunlight
R ough, scaly wings
I n the winter, their manes freeze
F erocious animals
F earless
O utstanding
N ot to be messed with.

Jackie Stewart (10)
Lochnell Primary School, Benderloch

All About Sqatier (Squid Crossed With A Cat Crossed With A Bear)

S o, so cute
Q ueen of all kind
A nd everyone obeys her
T he king is one of a kind
I love him to the moon and back
E ven when I'm gone
R ed, brown and pink.

Charlie Randle (8)
Lochnell Primary School, Benderloch

The Awkward Whale

I am a whale
I have a big tail
I am half-dragon
And have a big wagon
I am also a male

I am pretty fat
I also like a cat
I am lazy
But also very crazy
I am a big brat.

Mia Taylor (10)
Lochnell Primary School, Benderloch

My Pet Rabbit

R acing, but cute animals
A dorable creatures
B iting is what they do
B ut they are cute too
I love them all
T op to toe
S o fun they are!

Lucy Macgregor (9)
Lochnell Primary School, Benderloch

Mary The Beast

M ary, the marvellous beast
A lways stood on the edge of the forest, I think that was her home
R arely it has a big feast
Y ou can tell its home is not the shape of a dome.

Ashley Wood (11)
Lochnell Primary School, Benderloch

Ligon, The Lion Dragon

Ligon the lazy
Ligon the loving
He likes to be adorable
He likes to be cute
His mane is so fluffy
His mane is so cuddly
He is kind and friendly...
To the ones in his trust.

Rory Struthers (9)
Lochnell Primary School, Benderloch

Marlo

M iraculously strong
A stonishing speed
R esting a lot, sleeping in bed
L etting children play with his toys
O ffering food to people.

Finlay MacCallum (11)
Lochnell Primary School, Benderloch

Doge

My long-necked doggo
Wiggling in the summer trees
Eating all the leaves
He likes to play fetch
And play with me.

Fraser MacGregor (10)
Lochnell Primary School, Benderloch

Catibh Alaska

C ute, with very big button eyes
A nd an array of spots
T o be so cute would be amazing
I n his dreams, he would be Supercat
B ig paws with sharp claws
H e loves it when you hug him

A s well as his spots, he also has stripes on his head
L azy all the time
A mazing how long he can sleep for
S ledging is his favourite thing
K ind and big-hearted
A best friend for life.

Eevie Mackay (11)
Melvich Primary School, Melvich

Bulldog

B ulldogs
U sually
L ook
L ike
D ogs
O r
G oats.

Callan Mackay (10)
Melvich Primary School, Melvich

Wonder Cat

Wonder Cat is a scary, brave female
With a smooth and messy tail
She is teal, purple, blue and green
Her powers are fantastic
She can jump very high
As high as Big Ben
And fly in the sky
She's as fast as a blink of an eye
And as fat as a piggy
She can hit people in the head so fast
So look out for Wonder Cat
I ride on her back and save the whole world
And when we get home from my hero duty
We have pizza and cake
Then we go to bed
In the morning, we have the day off
So we get ready to go in the big pool
And have so much fun.

Leah MacPherson (9)
Portlethen Primary School, Portlethen

Pugosaur

P ugosaur is a friendly, fantastic, terrifying and gigantic dinosaur
U se your food quickly or Pugosaur will devour your whole fridge or worse, eat your whole house
G reat white teeth and likes to go on walks
O ff he goes to his bed, sleeping like a baby
S uddenly, he wakes up
A nd yawns as loud as a rocket
U nder your bed, you may see him and he waves his right paw
R ace him and you will lose instantly.

Caleb Bremner (10)
Portlethen Primary School, Portlethen

Dinochick

D inochick is very grumpy
I n the winter, Dinochick has to camouflage
N aturally green head, white teeth and orange body
O nly in the winter Dinochick hides
C limbs onto every tree when she's angry
H uge body and head
I sn't happy ever, Dinochick is always bad-tempered
C lever but is shy
K icks anyone who is cruel to Dinochick.

Mia Vaughan (9)
Portlethen Primary School, Portlethen

The Owlphant

O wlphants live on trees and on sand
W ater from the lake is very good for them
L arge animals can eat the owlphant but the owlphant has powers
P ineapples are what they eat
H is superpowers are running quickly, flying and jumping high up
A nts could be their food too
N ature for the owlphant is beautiful
T he forest is where they live.

Paulina Kekenmejster (10)
Portlethen Primary School, Portlethen

Catacorn

C atacorn is sweet, fluffy and adorable
A ll morning, she is running in the garden
T ill I wake up, she is scratching on my door
A fter lunch, Catacorn and me go to the park
C atacorn can also fly and has a horn
O n our way home, we saw a rainbow
R ight after we saw the rainbow, we ran home
N ow we got home, we jumped into our beds.

Jessica Hope Murray (8)
Portlethen Primary School, Portlethen

Sporty Snake

S kilful at every sport
P eople call him competitive
O ranges are his favourite food
R eally fast
T he colour red is his favourite
Y ou'll be impressed when you see him

S caly skin
N ever negative
A lways plays a sport
K ind to everyone
E veryone likes Sporty Snake.

Logan Bonner (9)
Portlethen Primary School, Portlethen

Dogasus

D ogasus is very cute, but don't trust her
O n Friday, Dogasus gives kids five wishes
G ives people flights around the city
A ll night long, Dogasus is making wishes come true
S ometimes she turns rainbow colours
U p above the stars is where she lives
S ometimes we play fetch and afterwards, we cuddle.

Hannah Cowie (8)
Portlethen Primary School, Portlethen

Unikitty

U nikitty is a very kind kitty
N ot even one kitty is as magical
I don't think anyone has one
K itty is a very big troublemaker
I t always escapes out of the house
T iptoes out of her cage to
T ips over everything and breaks it
Y anks everything off the shelves.

Lotti Szigeti (9)
Portlethen Primary School, Portlethen

Dragonbee

D ragonbee is tiny
R ude and scary
A lways stinging people
G rumpy and miserable
O n houses, spying for people
N ext time watch out, Dragonbee has horns and sharp teeth
B eware, Dragonbee is red and black
E veryone is scared
E ven Dragonbee is scared!

Zuzanna Kalczynska (9)
Portlethen Primary School, Portlethen

Crabasaur

C rabasaur is my best friend
R are kind of tail
A really big head
B ats are his favourite snack
A wesome friend
S uper good at fighting
A nnoying when he snores
U nder his orange claws, he keeps his sweets
R eally good at football.

Ryan Stuart Lawie (8)
Portlethen Primary School, Portlethen

Phoenix

P owerful and strong
H orse riding is fun for her
O riginal type of bird
E xpert and smart
N atural in fire
I ncredible at powers
e **X** cited when they go to hibernate.

Eva Duminicel (9)
Portlethen Primary School, Portlethen

Waspy The Wasp

W aspy is a pleasant wasp
A nd I found Waspy, he was lost
S o I picked Waspy up, he was lovely
P rivate room for him, he's in a better mood
Y ard is Waspy's favourite place to be.

Liam Law (10)
Portlethen Primary School, Portlethen

Fly Pug

F lying pug in the sky
L aunching into the clouds
Y ellow cape makes pug fly

P ug is brown and fluffy
U p and down in the air
G inger ears and ginger paws.

Freddi Ferguson (9)
Portlethen Primary School, Portlethen

Rocky The Dog

Rocky the dog is a weird dog
He can camouflage in rocks and mountains
It is exciting when we go on walks
Because he hides in the mountains
And makes me laugh
He is black and white and spotty.

Rockland Brooks (9)
Portlethen Primary School, Portlethen

Sporty The Dog

S ilent Sporty plays sports
P atient and stealthy
O nly one in the world
R ecord-breaking dog
T he sporty dog is very tough
Y oung and healthy dog.

Adi Pazio (9)
Portlethen Primary School, Portlethen

Rowl

R owl lives in the woods
O ak trees are cosy
W ide, big eyes on his forehead
L ong tail like a rat.

Baxter Smith (9)
Portlethen Primary School, Portlethen

Cassy The Colourful Cat

C assy is my cat,
A s regular as a bat,
S he has a secret, however, she has wings and rainbow stripes!
S o, at night, I hold on tight as she flies away out of sight.
Y ou may be thinking where do we go? Well, we go to a crystal cove.

T hen, when morning comes, we fly back home.
H ad we been caught? No, not yet.
E ither way, secret or public, we have fun flying through the sky

C assy and I have a special relationship like no other cat and human.
A t home, we act normal but now you know what really happens.
T o fly up high, it takes great power. Who knows? I still wonder.

Haadiya Omar (9)
Ridgeway Farm CE Academy, Purton

Banana Bear

My bear isn't like any other,
I adopted him because he didn't have a mother.
He doesn't have any brothers
And he is obsessed with bananas.

I found out why he loved bananas,
He had to eat them to get superpowers.
I am lucky that I adopted him
And he eats a lot of bananas, so he isn't very slim.

Lots of villains want to capture him,
Like a giant bee or something crazy.
So now you know all about my bear,
If you see a bear, feed it bananas, then maybe it will become a...
Banana bear!

Yvette Ncube (9)
Ridgeway Farm CE Academy, Purton

Monty The Marvellous Monkey!

I have a marvellous pet,
His name is Monty
And he is a monkey!
Monty loves eating bananas,
But the bananas make him go *nuts!*
The bananas make Monty run everywhere,
But after he runs, he sleeps.

He has a cape, mask and...
Is a superhero (a marvellous one)!
He can fly as fast as a motorbike,
But at the end of the day,
He is my pet monkey,
He is cute and cuddly
And I love him!

Jaiyana Gurung (10)
Ridgeway Farm CE Academy, Purton

Magic Mouse

M agic Mouse liked to play, he
A lways made a thing out of clay,
G eorge liked to watch his tricks,
I t made him laugh and say, "Hooray!"
C ould he be a magician one day?

M agic Mouse went to bed, his bed was made
O ut of cheese,
U nder the bed, there was more cheese,
S tinky, smelly, pongy cheese,
E ating the cheese was Magic Mouse.

Max Bennett (10)
Ridgeway Farm CE Academy, Purton

Rocking Rabbit's Concert

I went to a concert,
Rocking Rabbit was on the stage,
The opening riff was heavy rock
And then he sang about a smelly sock,
His voice just screeched,
Like he had drunk some bleach,
It was long and hard,
Until he broke into a solo,
He went into another verse
And sang about a multiverse,
He finished with an ending chord
And everyone clapped and cheered.

Zubin Beach (9)
Ridgeway Farm CE Academy, Purton

Surf The Surfing Chicken

Surf is a surfer,
He loves the waves,
He has good balance
And is stylish too.

He never falls off
And is always at the beach,
He also makes good beats.

Surf is happy with his surfing life,
He's hardly ever off the splashing waves
And when he is off,
He is relaxing on his bed
With a nice cup of tea.

Erin Blackmore (9)
Ridgeway Farm CE Academy, Purton

My Llama Dog!

I have a little llama dog,
She is very funny!
She likes to eat bananas
And is very sassy

Her name is Bella,
She has black fur.
Whenever she barks,
You can always hear her!

She has long legs
And is very tall!
You would never think
She was small!

Kyra Morgan (10)
Ridgeway Farm CE Academy, Purton

Slockage The Slinky Dog

In a car far, far away,
There was a sausage dog that had a power, called Slinky.
He jumped over the window,
Extending his body out in London,
up Big Ben.
I pulled him back and then he went out the sunroof,
Driving past the London Eye,
He went on and stared at my eye...

Leo Clarke (10)
Ridgeway Farm CE Academy, Purton

Jenny The Jumping Gerbil

Jenny is my gerbil,
She likes to jump over hurdles!
She can jump high on a trampoline!

She jumps off windowsills and all those things,
It's almost like she has wings!
She jumps off beds and buildings too!
Sometimes she jumps over pools of goo!

Freya Blackmore (9)
Ridgeway Farm CE Academy, Purton

Moons, The Cat Of Planets

Moons is a cat
That flies up to space,
Waves goodbye from outer space,
Jumps up and down on the moon,
She likes to wear a jumpsuit,
She loves the planet Mars,
Goes there once a week,
Doesn't like to eat fruit,
But loves to eat meat.

Vittoria Dos Santos (10)
Ridgeway Farm CE Academy, Purton

Cyber The Chick

Hole in the wall?
What a weird thing.
What could've done it?
Such a peculiar thing.
My pet is a chick with laser eyes.
That's what could've done it.
That's right, his eyes!

Terrence French (9)
Ridgeway Farm CE Academy, Purton

Rocket The Rainbow Rabbit!

Rocket is a rabbit
Who likes eating cabbage
Can she have her own habits?
She keeps me warm with her fluffy fur
Eating carrots is what she does
Being tired is just her thing.

Freya Popovic (9)
Ridgeway Farm CE Academy, Purton

My Chunky Monkey

My chunky monkey
Is really grumpy
Sits in bed
Eating all the Cheerios
Must slap him on the head
Oh, how sad I am for slapping his head
Must give him a Band-Aid.

Tinotenda Mundembe (10)
Ridgeway Farm CE Academy, Purton

My Teleporting Turtle

My Teleporting Turtle teleports everywhere.
In the fridge, the garden and my bed.
He is terrified of talking tigers in bed,
So he teleports to the bath when he is terrified.

Max Keating Ladd (10)
Ridgeway Farm CE Academy, Purton

A Puppy

A tiny little puppy
A tiny little scruffy
Sometimes he loves to get a little smelly
Next time I will take him out
He will get a little muddy.

Freddie Hall (10)
Ridgeway Farm CE Academy, Purton

Rollie The Roller-Skating Hamster

Oh Rollie, Rollie
You're very, very noisy
I'm trying to sleep
Not even a peep
Just go to sleep
Oh, little Rollie.

Maisie Debs New (10)
Ridgeway Farm CE Academy, Purton

Cute Koala

As kind as me
Very loving
As clever as me
As lazy as my brother
As cute as a baby.

Harry Stoddart (10)
Ridgeway Farm CE Academy, Purton

Vicious Giant Dogs

V ery scary, violent dog
I cannot believe what I saw
C lawed feet and paws
I was very afraid
O pening the door to release a demon
U nleashing a terrible monster
S tarbucks had to wait

G uards were called to the growling noise
I couldn't believe it
A mazed, the teenagers stood like statues
N o escape for the monster
T he army overpower the monster

D are it escape?
O h my goodness, I was so terrified
G iant dog takes 20 years to repair
S o it can exact its revenge, you're in for a scare

Daniel Legan (13)
Rutherglen High School, Campus Lane

Simba

S peedy, super strength
I nfra-red vision
M ighty paws
B ody of steel
"A rgh!" shouts everyone.

Euan Shevlin (13)
Rutherglen High School, Campus Lane

The Fart Knight

My friend Critch is very friendly
But she tries to hide her identity
She learned martial farts
So get ready, villains, you'll shout in fear
To smell what's up Critch's rear!
She is the Fart Knight.
Her other movies: Pooper Man Vs The Fart Knight,
The Fart Knight 1,
The Fart Knight 2.

Conor McGarry (10)
St Joseph's Primary School, Antrim

Loki Poki

Loki Poki is my dog, once he ate a hedgehog!
When he went into the woods, he found something very good,
The thing he found was in the ground
It was a whopping two pounds,
He brought it back to you after he took a poo,
Then I walked down the street to buy a little treat.

Lucius McCollum (11)
St Joseph's Primary School, Antrim

Dogsaurus

I have a pet dogsaurus
Her name is Rosesaurus
She doesn't like staying indoors
If she doesn't get a banana
She will attack you
She sometimes forgets
Where the toilet is
And goes to the toilet in my bedroom
Then she starts farting and I said, "Eww!"
Then she got mad and ate my fish, Tony.

Melissa Nicolson (9)
Westray Junior High School, Westray

The Tale Of Stevie Saurus

One bonny day, I went out for a walk
I met the pet of my dreams
Orange with black spots
And a horn, big ears and two wings
She is called Stevie Saurus

I took her home and let her fly
She turned out to be rather shy
I made a treehouse
And she didn't leave my finger
She is mine forever.

Mia Pottinger (9)
Westray Junior High School, Westray

The Most Peculiar Pet

I love my little Noomacorn
I love her, oh so much
I love my little Noomacorn
But her real name is Chusk
She's the one and only
She's the best of all
She loves being tall
She loves her new friend, Paul
When I call for bedtime
She comes in like a horse
She loves bedtime.

Eiza Dickinson (8)
Westray Junior High School, Westray

Meindy

Once in the night, I found
A bat called Meindy
I kept him as a pet
He mind-controlled me
And made me go to his cave

I was mind-blown
Meindy stopped
Mind-controlling me
I was amazed at
How beautiful his cave was.

Arun Summers (7)
Westray Junior High School, Westray

Pokat

Grace is always cheery
Her house is a bit eerie
She loves Katy Perry
On her nose are berries

Grace doesn't like making tarts
In case she farts
She has something wrong with her heart
Because she got hit by a dart.

Tanna Groat (9)
Westray Junior High School, Westray

The Silliest Pig-Pog

I have a pig-pog
It likes to dig
Even if it is big
It likes to play with wigs
If it gets stuck in the muck
When it plays
Every so often
I climb on my pig-pog
After I'm on it
It flies away.

Millie-Megan Bliss (7)
Westray Junior High School, Westray

Messi Monster

M essi is a boy like Lionel Messi, the football superstar
E xtraordinary speed for a mutated animal
S o, Messi is very good at football, of course
S cales like a big fish
I love Messi.

Stewart Rendall (8)
Westray Junior High School, Westray

Gary's Friends

G ary is gigantic with a big nose and tall ears
A pples are his favourite fruit to munch with a deer
R oadrunner is his best pal
Y ou might see them running past the canal.

Robert Sam Rendall (9)
Westray Junior High School, Westray

The Fishasaurus Eats Broccoli

B etsy likes to eat big fish
E very single day
T eatime, she eats broccoli
S he then goes out to play
Y ay! It's bedtime and another day the morn.

Mason Bain (8)
Westray Junior High School, Westray

Wayne, The Duck-Billed Snakeapus

W ayne has met Harry Kane
A nd he is a duck-billed snakeapus
Y ou should run away from him
N ever eats fish, only crocodile
E verybody knows Wayne.

James Groat (7)
Westray Junior High School, Westray

Mr Pringle, The Perfect Dog

Every night, I dream of being with a 'pawfect pug' with biscuit eyes and a chubby tummy I can hug!
He helps me solve maths puzzles
By pointing to answers with his flat muzzle
We spend hours splashing in the puddles,
Its wrinkly face beaming as it jumps at me for cuddles!
In my dreams, he plays ping-pong with his stubby paws,
While drinking his bubble tea with paper straws!
Looking lovely in his star pyjamas,
He pops Pringles while watching a show on llamas!
I imagine him clutching to me as I walk out the door,
Wagging his tail, dancing hips when I'm back from school at four!
One day, my dream will come true,
When I will introduce to you,

My peculiar, pawfect pug, 'Mr Pringle'!

Shiv Vohra (7)
Wetherby School, London

My White Horse Galope

M y very special pet horse is called Galope.
Y ummy grass is his favourite snack.

H appily, he runs when we tell him to.
O utside, he feels the happiest.
R ivers and fields, he can cross anything.
S unny day or rainy day, he always wants to play.
E legant horse never gives up.

G alope is called Galope because that's how we say 'gallop' in Portugese.
A mazing horse can do anything.
L iking everybody, he makes us happy.
O h gosh, he is great!
P olite, gentle and calm, he doesn't annoy anyone.
E nd of the day, he sleeps standing.

Pedro Aboim (7)
Wetherby School, London

Cheeky Leopard

L urking leopards like mine scare me when I'm outside, I like it a lot but it kind of scares me!
E ating anything that is in the forest, desert and savannah is his delight.
O il is what my leopard doesn't like, when he sees it, he'll run away as fast as he can!
P awing paws is the best thing, his feet are quiet wherever we go!
A ll of my spots on my luxury leopard are identical and I love them that way.
R ad leopards are not as good as mine, they might do things better but he is still the best cheeky leopard.
D ark nights are great, I can see how much the leopard's eyes can glow!

Dhilan Besser (7)
Wetherby School, London

A Sassy, Slimy And Slithery Pet

My enormous pet lives in a giant fish tank,
When it sleeps, it likes to lie on the sandbank.

Like a lion or leopard, it is a carnivore, eating fish,
Rays and shark being the favourite dish.

Looking ferocious with fiery eyes and shiny scales,
All in all, its length is six metres from head to tail.

Out in nature, its habitat is salty waters close to the shore,
It catches its prey silently, without a roar.

Any animal can be a pet,
As long as it is well kept.

Now I want to make you smile,
My favourite pet is a saltwater crocodile.

Raphael Zechner (7)
Wetherby School, London

Panmoncroc Bat

P anmoncroc Bats are stealthy, so beware!
A nimals found in many habitats, land, sea and air!
N ow they are endangered
M iles high or miles low they're happy to go
O mnivore craving, especially for ice cream
N octurnal the older are.
C an you believe the mouth is as small as a chihuahua?
R oars as loud as a lion!
O h! But don't be afraid... They
C an't eat humans.

B lack shiny coats
A re what hunters want
T rouble they are in.

Sebastian Zacharioudakis (7)
Wetherby School, London

The Flying Fleece
Based on the Flying Fleece, Ambleside

Gazing up at the field, I spot a cotton-wool dot.
Is it a sheep or a flying fleece?
Take a peep and check it's not those pesky geese.
It's hardly mute,
But it's still really cute.
It bleats out a 'maa!'
Most commonly known as an ear-splitting 'baa!'
Rounded up swiftly by the sheepdog,
Even when the hills are misty and covered in fog.
The same as the others, but with two extra things,
A pair of fine gold-plated wings.
Oh, how I love my furry, festive, flying fleece!

Jack-Li Woon (7)
Wetherby School, London

Hot Dog Hound

It was in the park where I had found
My super, amazing hot dog hound.
His fur was as light as a hot dog's bun,
His eyes were as bright as the shimmery sun!
I took him home to give him a bath,
He jumped all around and it did make us laugh!
He didn't like the hoover, not one bit at all,
I thought he would curl up into a ball!
Instead, in a fiery flash, he turned
Into a hot dog when scared, I learned!
This just made him more perfect to me,
Best friends forever we always shall be.

Lucas Marks (7)
Wetherby School, London

My Peculiar Pet

D own the straight street strolled a strange dog as strange as an awkward alien
O nly it was as furry and ferocious as a dangerous tiger and as
B eautiful and marvellous as a butterfly
B ut can be as dangerous as a shiny shark
Y et has a big nose like the more of a proboscis messy monkey, with

D umbo-like ears so he can fly right up to the magical moon
O f course, we can't forget the gorgeous, god-like
G azelle's horrifying horns.

Izaia Porseous (7)
Wetherby School, London

The Albatdeer

A ntlers on top of a soft feathery face
L egs like long rulers with hooves at the tip
B ut wings that seem as wide as the world
A lbert the Albatdeer is my best friend.
'T was a starry night when I met him as he lay his body next to my tent
D ear Albert was tired and his snoring woke me up
E xtraordinary he looked, snuggling into my tent
E nthusiastically, he tucked into the food I shared
R eal friends we are and that we will be.

Sebastian Lavers (7)
Wetherby School, London

My Peculiar Pet

B linky Blink is a very special pet
L unch is what he needs
I t loves swimming super fast
N ot one person doesn't want it
K umquat is its favourite food
Y olk is its favourite thing for breakfast

B oats are its favourite vehicle
L ooking like an eagle, it stares at you every day
I t is tired after lunch
N ot a peep you hear from it when it is sleeping
K indly, it sets the table.

Alexander Grimm (7)
Wetherby School, London

The Peculiar Working Dog

The dog has volumes of hair,
Which most times dropped on the itchy chair.
Working Dog rides to his office on a scooter,
When he gets in, he sets up his computer!
When there's a blazing storm,
Working Dog's ears become as pointy as a horn.
His cute, round, blue eyes
Often are as adorable as butterflies.
Working Dog is extremely clever,
Except when he runs, he becomes even redder.
But I love him all the same
And he is very easy to entertain.

Federico Assetto (7)
Wetherby School, London

Bolterone

B old and strong, my super dog is never wrong.
O range, green and yellow, he's a big fellow who lives on marshmallows.
L ong legs help him run fast and beat a jet plane in a blast!
T ogether we make the world better!
E very step he takes makes his enemies shake.
R eliable and likeable
O pinionated and always excited.
N ot a day with him goes without play.
E nd of story! He is a dog full of glory.

Sam Chebaklo (6)
Wetherby School, London

My Flying Cat

M aking mayhem all the time.
Y ellow crazy cat.

F eathers sprouting from her white wings.
L ong furry tail to balance.
Y elling when it's time for dinner.
I love my crazy cat.
N obody can catch her.
G reat, big, long claws for scratching.

C laws get stuck to carpets and clothes.
A ttacking birds and insects.
T ail swishing from side to side.

Henry Abraham (7)
Wetherby School, London

Milo The Irritating Millipede

M ilo is my millipede,
I n his mind, he thinks he's a lean, mean, munching machine,
L ike a hungry wolf,
L icking his lips with glory,
I n fact, I call him Mr Cuty.
P S Milo doesn't like it,
E very day he tries to munch me
D ear oh dear, I would say, "Stop being so irritating Milo,"
E very hour, "Stop being so irritating, stop being so irritating..."

Leo Head (7)
Wetherby School, London

My Marvellous Cat

Yesterday, I adopted a very cute cat,
I even bought it a lovely, nice hat,
It is brown and cuddly like a log,
It sometimes gets stuck in a bog
The peculiar thing about this lovely pet
Is that it has a tail as long as the vets!
Its eyes are bright, deep blue
And it has really smelly poo!
Everybody says he is weird
Except a man with a beard,
But I say he is most perfect
And that's what matters.

Wenty Beaumont (7)
Wetherby School, London

Leonidas

L eonidas is a peculiar pet.
E nergetically, he pounces on his delicious prey.
O n top of a rock, he likes to gaze at the vast open land.
N aughty and cheeky for much of the time.
I n and out of the roads he frolics with his friends.
D own from the sky, he glides gracefully like a sparrow.
A dapted to nature he is all the time.
S eldom does he get in a rage and roar.

Epaminondas George Embiricos (7)
Wetherby School, London

Pretzy Pet

P retzy Pet is my special pet
R are and precious like a diamond.
E very time I feed him, he gives a lick.
T remendous like a super stick
Z igzags through the trees all day
Y senburg is his second name.

P ets are everywhere, but not this one
E xcept when meeting the middle one.
T ristan is my name and I love my Pretzy Pet.

Tristan Ysenburg (7)
Wetherby School, London

The Sea Dragon

F lame is a very rare species.
L eeches are what he eats, that's why he lives in the forest as big as the sea.
A s I sleep, he goes in the sea and swims with the whales and dolphins.
M essages pop up from his head, I am a fortune-teller, I can understand.
E merging from his cave, he stays like a grown-up and never gets old, that's what makes him my special pet.

Leo Larsson (7)
Wetherby School, London

Slinky Winky Woo

There once was a dog called Slinky
Who was as stretchy as could be,
He was not like any other dog,
It was quite extraordinary.

He could reach up to the sky,
Taller than an aeroplane could fly
And wink as he came down
Slinking to the ground.

He was incredibly adorable,
Well, that's what the girls would say,
When I took him out each and
Every day.

Teddy Lazari (7)
Wetherby School, London

My Brilliant Pet Drago

My ferocious pet Drago can fly and fight
My dangerous pet Drago is like dynamite
He doesn't need to eat
All he needs is sleep
My brilliant pet Drago can create fire and light

My clever pet Drago can be big or small
My flexible pet Drago can curl into a ball
He can fit in my pocket
And can power a rocket.
My peculiar pet Drago is the best of them all.

Freddie Jilla (7)
Wetherby School, London

Hilarious Herbert

H ilarious Herbert munching happily.
E asily eating scrumptious broccoli quickly.
R avenous Herbert ate his amazing food.
B ouncing up and down, Herbert ran around the room excitedly.
E very day, Herbert had his daily wonderful walk.
R apidly, Herbert zoomed to the glorious garden.
T he sun goes down as Herbert rushes inside insanely.

Alexander Michael Haddad (7)
Wetherby School, London

Invisicat

I nvisicat is my invisible pet
N ight-time is when it starts to catch mice.
V acant is the kitchen at that time
I t lives in my room
S its and relaxes on my bed
I t goes out at 12am
C lawed paws, they kill mice
A t 7am, it comes back and wakes me up
T ick-tock, it's time for Invisicat's nap.

Farrukh Sheikh (7)
Wetherby School, London

My Peculiar Pet

S ausage Dog is weird
A nd should be feared
U nless you are Bartle
S o you have been warned!
A nd you would be startled
G rumble and tremble
E very day, but you have been warned.

D ogs like these are very rare
O f course, you must treat them with care.
G o and see but beware.

Bartle Frankopan
Wetherby School, London

Truffle Dog

T ruffle is my favourite dog, he sits on a log.
R unning and jumping is what he loves and does.
U mbrellas are his favourite weapon I reckon.
F ighting all day long is his song.
F un and games are his name.
L icking is cute and he sounds like a toot.
E ars are his sensors and they guide him to Marks and Spencers!

Lucas Zammitt (7)
Wetherby School, London

Splash

S plash is my glistening goldfish
P lenty of fish favour him as the friendliest of all
L ingering about, he is always blissfully bored
A stonishingly, he can turn into any marine animal
S ometimes he's a wistful whale, sometimes he's a shiny shrimp
H e's always using his perplexing power, would you like to see?

Rupert Nicholls (7)
Wetherby School, London

The Giraffe With No Neck

C owaffe has the name of a giraffe
O MG, it has no neck.
W ild, it lives in Africa.
R ed eyes and spots make it colourful.
A t dawn, ferocious lions strolled by,
F unny frogs jumped about.
F aster than fast, Cowraffe ran.
E vading the lions, he hid like a zebra.

Billy Marsh (7)
Wetherby School, London

Peculiar Pets

Miky was a hungry mouse
His tummy was as big as a house
It might surprise you all to hear
For lunch his food is deer
Nibble, nibble, munch, munch,
Nibble, nibble, munch,
Nibble, nibble, munch, munch
A deer for lunch!
Miky was big, Miky was numb
Miky had a very big tum.

Hamzah Sharaf (6)
Wetherby School, London

My Special Bulldog

B ulldog, my peculiar pet
U nder the sun, he sleeps till lunch
L ater, he gives me a paw and woof woofs
L and is the best, my dog does not like to get wet
D angerous? No no, he's shy
O lympic Bulldog is a star on stage
G enius Bulldog is the best.

Conrad Parkin (6)
Wetherby School, London

Toitoi My Pet

T imidly, tiresome Toitoi hides from a doggy
O ptimistic and hopeful, Toitoi never gets sold
I ncredibly slow, as slow as a snail
T oitoi munches on yummy lettuce
O n the way to the other end of the cage she sleeps
I ncredible Toitoi finds some leftover food.

Edward Abboud (7)
Wetherby School, London

Shadow

J umping out of dark shadows
A ttacking all its prey
G reat, majestic, beautiful and stealthy is my pet.
U nder the garden bushes is his whole world
A lmost no one knows he is all mine
R eturning Shadow to the jungle is my one day's wish!

Xander Petersen (7)
Wetherby School, London

Raurus

My mumma brought home a dinosaur
She said she found it by the seashore
He was the great ankylosaurus
So I named him Raurus
His eyes and body were very funny
And he was always in a hurry
Raurus was kind, caring and not scary
He became my pet and was merry.

Yuveer Goenka (7)
Wetherby School, London

Tosca Is Cheeky

T osca, Tosca, let me sleep just one more glorious hour.
O h no, Tosca, you spilt the water, Mama's going to go mental.
S oftly, Tosca cuddles up with the fluffiest tail in the world.
C ats are always lovely
A nd are always in your bed.

Alex Taylor (7)
Wetherby School, London

My Dream Lizard

My dream lizard
Is small and scaly.
He is fast, noisy, funny and crazy.

He has bright, shiny
Turquoise eyes
And a long tongue
To catch flies.

My dream lizard lives in a cage
On my desk
And he is my very
Best friend.

Philip Teboul (7)
Wetherby School, London

Sky The Goldfish

I have a fish called Sky,
She always swims by,
She is orange and smiley
And jumps around wildly!

She swims all day
And only wants to play
I would swim with her if I had...
My way.
I love goldfish,
Finally, I got my wish!

Maxi Fatemi (7)
Wetherby School, London

The Best Dog!

I have a dog who hugs all the time
He never walks, he jumps or runs!
When I go to school,
He dances around in the street
And hops on my scooter to do some tricks!
But he is scared of the colour purple.
When he sees it, he hugs me tight.

Alexander Whyatt (7)
Wetherby School, London

My Pet

P ant! She is here, the best day ever!
E verybody fear Super Pepper.
P epper's the best dog ever, so beware.
P hew! Everyone is saved!
E veryone, beware!
"R uff!" Run away, baddies.

Rex Richardson (7)
Wetherby School, London

Girtt

G reat Girtt appears from nowhere
I n the sun or rain, you can't tell
R ed he is like an angry Swiss bull,
T owering above the clouds, he's never seen,
T hough he likes to gobble up teens.

Arthur Lindback (7)
Wetherby School, London

Batty-Bat's Information

I had a pet called Batty-Bat
No one has him and he sits on a mat.
He occasionally wears a hat,
He is friends with a rat called Matt
And is enemies with a cat.
He also has a watch
He waves with a swat.

Theo Gladkov (6)
Wetherby School, London

The One And Only Yeyo!

Y eyo, my pet labrador, gives me his big, black, heavy paw,
E ach time I stroke him, he sometimes growls,
Y elp, yelp, he howls
O ver and over from his drooling jowls!

Eduardo Rio (7)
Wetherby School, London

Sneaky

S erves ice cream
N o one has Sneaky, it's my special pet
E very night he flies
A lways catches squid
K ind to everyone
Y ellow beak.

Hugh Crossley Wright (7)
Wetherby School, London

Pandemic Pup

Daisy my dachshund
She thinks she's a rooster
She crows when she barks
Oh my, she thinks she can fly
She's a superhero dog
That looks a bit like a log.

Freddy Bakewell (6)
Wetherby School, London

YOUNG WRITERS INFORMATION

We hope you have enjoyed reading this book – and that you will continue to in the coming years.

If you're a young writer who enjoys reading and creative writing, or the parent of an enthusiastic poet or story writer, visit our website www.youngwriters.co.uk/subscribe to join the World of Young Writers and receive news, competitions, writing challenges, tips, articles and giveaways! There is lots to keep budding writers motivated to write!

If you would like to order further copies of this book, or any of our other titles, then please give us a call or order via your online account.

Young Writers
Remus House
Coltsfoot Drive
Peterborough
PE2 9BF
(01733) 890066
info@youngwriters.co.uk

Join in the conversation!
Tips, news, giveaways and much more!

 **YoungWritersUK**   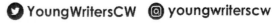 **YoungWritersCW**   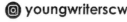 **youngwriterscw**